18th-Century Fashion in Detail

Susan North

Photographs by Henrietta Clare
and Richard Davis
Drawings by Leonie Davis
and Deborah Mallinson

Thames
&Hudson | V&A

Frontispiece:
A man's court dress coat and waistcoat of embroidered
velvet and silk, French, 1780s–90s
Bequeathed by C. A. Beavan
T.231&A-1917

First published in the United Kingdom in 1998 by
the Victoria and Albert Museum, London

This revised and expanded edition first published in the United
Kingdom in 2018 by Thames & Hudson Ltd, 181A High Holborn,
London WC1V 7QX, in association with the Victoria and Albert
Museum, London

This revised and expanded edition first published in the United
States of America in 2018 in by Thames & Hudson Inc.,
500 Fifth Avenue, New York, New York 10110

Reprinted 2024

18th-Century Fashion in Detail © 2018 Victoria and Albert
Museum, London/Thames & Hudson Ltd, London

Text, V&A photographs and line illustrations
© 2018 Victoria and Albert Museum, London
Design and layout © 2018 Thames & Hudson Ltd, London

British Library Cataloguing-in-Publication Data
A catalogue record for this book is available from
the British Library

Library of Congress Control Number 2017959305

ISBN 978-0-500-29263-1

Printed and bound in China by
Shenzhen Reliance Printing Co. Ltd

MIX
Paper from
responsible sources
FSC® C102842
www.fsc.org

Be the first to know about our new releases,
exclusive content and author events by visiting
thamesandhudson.com
thamesandhudsonusa.com
thamesandhudson.com.au

V&A Publishing
Supporting the world's leading
museum of art and design,
the Victoria and Albert
Museum, London

Historical Fashion in Detail, co-authored with Avril Hart,
was published by the Victoria and Albert Museum in
1998, following the successful first volume of the
series *Modern Fashion in Detail*. The 'Fashion in Detail'
series has been relaunched and eighteenth-century
fashion now has its own volume, with an introduction
to eighteenth-century dress and 137 objects from
the V&A's collections. More than half of these are new
– with photographs, line drawings and descriptions –
and those that appeared in *Historical Fashion in Detail*
have been updated with new research. The original
hand-drawn diagrams have been complemented
by new digital drawings.

Contents

18th-Century
Fashion in Detail

INTRODUCTION

Dressing fashionably was a very different process in the eighteenth century from what it is now. Eighteenth-century dress was governed by a strict etiquette of what was worn at particular times of the day in various social circumstances. It was crucial not only to be wearing the latest styles but to be seen in them at the proper time and in the right place.[1] Being fashionable required careful scrutiny of the clothing worn by one's contemporaries on different occasions. Illustrations of new styles only became available in the form of pocket-book plates after 1759 and fashion plates after 1770. These were available in limited numbers and were not widely distributed, so keeping up with contemporary fashion required observation and consultation with friends and makers.[2] Family and friends travelling to fashion centres such as London and Paris were instructed to look closely and send back descriptions of the latest styles.[3]

France dominated the fashion industries, and its influence can be seen in the textiles or styles – or both – of most eighteenth-century British garments, as well as in reactions, occasionally, against its decrees. London was the centre of sartorial excellence in Britain, having the greatest concentration of the fashion and textile trades, and the processes of acquiring the most stylish items of dress can be determined from three texts that describe these occupations. *The London Tradesman* (1747), *A General Description of all Trades* (1747) and *The Parent's and Guardian's Directory* (1761) explained who made fashionable fabrics and dress, as well as what skills were required, the price of an apprenticeship, the cost of setting up a business, and the status of each craft or trade in a complicated hierarchy of British industry.

For most of the eighteenth century, fashionable dress for women came in three main styles: the mantua, sack and gown (left). Only in the 1770s did new styles and variations of these appear. The three-piece suit of coat, waistcoat and breeches (page 8) was the foundation of all men's clothing, with varieties of fabric and subtle details of cut indicating degrees of formality. The elements of fashion that changed over the century for men and women were primarily the silhouette and decoration of dress, and, most importantly, the textiles and trimmings from which items were made. While this range of garments seems limited, eighteenth-century fashion offered a wide choice in the appearance of a new ensemble and required a series of decisions about fabrics and decoration, as well as overall style. New fashions were the result of collaborations between purchasers and a range of craftspeople, and selections from a wide assortment of materials made in a variety of techniques, created in harmony with the aesthetic principles of the age. The latest style included not only the shape and cut of a garment, but also the design of the fabric of which it was made and the decorations applied to it. The first step for customers in search of the latest style of clothing was to purchase the fabric and trimmings they desired (opposite). Although only the five natural fibres – silk, wool, linen, hemp and cotton – were available in the eighteenth century, they produced a remarkable variety of textiles suitable for fashionable dress.

The Silk Mercer

Silk was the most expensive and luxurious of textiles, desired for its sheen, its ability to hold dyes of brilliant colour and the intricate patterns that could be worked into its weave. Court and formal evening dress for British men and women was made of silk, and many elite women wore silk garments during the day. In the eighteenth century, silks were purchased from a silk mercer. The trade card of the silk mercers Dare and Hitchcock (see page 8, above left) lists the typical selection of brocades, damasks, lustrings, sarsenets, satins and velvets available in London in the middle of the century. The silks on offer would have been either imported from France or Italy or woven in Britain. Varieties of plain silks and silk blends were woven in Norwich, Canterbury, Paisley and Dublin, but Spitalfields in London was the centre of production for patterned silks.[4]

Although influenced by the latest French designs, Spitalfields developed its own distinctly British style in the 1740s and 1750s, and the industry was described in one trade manual as 'a very ingenious business ... greatly exceeding in their richness and the beauty of the patterns, those made in France'.[5]

The high price of eighteenth-century silks was due to the cost of the raw silk and the time and labour required to convert it into thread and to weave it. The greater the amount or weight of silk in a finished fabric, the higher the price; the more complex its weave, the higher the cost of labour. Silks woven with silver or silver-gilt thread (see pages 26, 186 and 209) were the most expensive. The dense silk pile of velvets (see pages 74 and 211) consumed five to seven times as much thread as a plain silk, and a complex cut and uncut design (see page 138) demanded particular skills of the weaver and added to the price.[6] Silks with complex weave structures or patterns usually demanded additional skills and labour: the drawing and technical expertise of a designer, more time and different techniques from the weaver, and the work of at least one additional person on the loom. Plain silks came in a variety of weights – from the solid ribbed weave of the waistcoat on page 204 to the fine lustring of the silk domino on page 172 – which would also affect their price.

In the hierarchy of London trades, mercers ranked with goldsmiths in prestige, and they required considerable wealth in order to set up shop. According to one trade manual, a minimum of £10,000 was needed to invest in a stock of luxurious silks to offer customers, and a successful mercer required a good eye and familiarity with the latest designs.[7] 'A thorough knowledge of the nature, properties, and difference between the several kinds of Silks' and 'a general knowledge of the manner of weaving' were considered essential.[8] Mercers were the intermediaries between the weavers, from whom they ordered their silks, and their customers. They conveyed the tastes and preferences of the latter to the former and introduced purchasers to the latest patterns.[9] As the trade card above demonstrates, some mercers also sold wool–silk blends such as bombazeen and poplin, as well as some of the more expensive stuff (wool) damasks.

The Woollen Draper

Fabrics made of wool were sold by woollen drapers. Of the eighteenth-century dress that survives, wool is found mainly in men's garments, but inventories and other records of women's dress indicate that a range of wool fabrics were used for their clothing too.[10] Wool had been Britain's primary textile manufacture since

ABOVE LEFT Trade card of Dare and Hitchcock, Mercers, c. 1740–60.

ABOVE The 18th-century man's suit: coat, waistcoat, breeches
T.137–1932

PREVIOUS PAGES, LEFT Detail of a copy of a plate engraved by Noël Le Mire after Gravelot, published in 1764

PREVIOUS PAGES, RIGHT The three main styles of 18th-century women's dress from top: mantua, sack, gown
T.324–1985, T.426–1990, T.433–1967

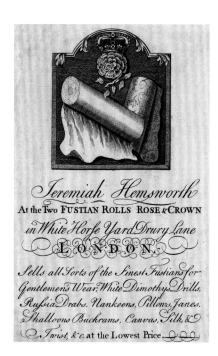

Trade card of Jeremiah Hemsworth, linen draper, c. 1725–50

the Middle Ages, and in the eighteenth century production expanded in Britain, particularly in the finer woollens that were made into both formal and informal suits worn by middle-class, gentry and aristocratic men.[11] The two main varieties in surviving dress are woollen and worsted. The former was woven, fulled or shrunk to tighten the weave, and then brushed with teasles to pull out the fibres and create a nap. This was sheared off and the process repeated until the weave was almost completely obscured and the surface of the fabric was thick and soft (see page 21). Produced in wider widths than other woollen fabrics, it was known as broadcloth. Woollen drapers usually bought their broadcloths white and had them dyed in fashionable colours, an investment that could cost up to £5,000.[12]

The other type of wool fabric was worsted, which was tightly woven with a smooth, shiny yarn that created a dense, almost waterproof fabric (see page 53, above). Worsted was often used for outer garments, such as men's and women's riding clothes and men's greatcoats (overcoats).

The Linen Draper

Eighteenth-century fashion required a wide range of linen fabrics, and these were supplied by linen drapers (left). The finest and sheerest linens were used for accessories (see page 111). Men's shirts, women's shifts and dressing jackets were made from finely spun, densely woven linens (see pages 33, below and 85, above), while a coarser version was used for items such as the hoop petticoat on page 85, below. Other types of linen formed the foundations of stays (see page 33) and lined the bodices of the different styles of women's dress. Buckram, made of linen stiffened with glue, reinforced the shape of men's coats, waistcoats and women's riding habits. The sign of the linen draper whose card is shown left was 'two fustian rolls'. Fustian was a blend of linen warp and cotton weft used for the linings of waistcoats.

Although linen had been produced in Britain for centuries, the finest and most fashionable varieties were the hollands, cambrics and lawns woven in the Low Countries. In the eighteenth century the British government promoted and encouraged linen production in Ireland and Scotland in order to compete with European imports.[13] Linen drapers' inventories included a range of both hemp and flax textiles produced in Ireland, Scotland and England, as well as the fine linens from Holland and France and coarser, cheaper varieties from Germany.[14] To provide such varieties, a linen draper required '£900 to £1,000 to set up master in a genteel retail shop'.[15]

Included in a draper's wares were the many cotton fabrics imported from India. In the eighteenth century, however, these were never referred to as 'cottons', a word used for a coarse type of wool.[16] The Indian textile exports were described collectively as 'calicos', although each type had its own name, for example muslin.[17] These imports first became widely available in the seventeenth century via the British East India Company, in a variety of plain fabrics, from fine muslin to heavy-duty dungaree, as well as the brilliantly dyed and patterned chintzes. The latter proved so popular that they were considered a threat to the native silk and wool industries, and between 1721 and 1774 all printed or decoratively dyed cotton fabrics – no matter where they were produced – were banned in Britain.[18] Plain white cottons were not affected by the chintz ban, and the fine Indian muslins continued to be made into accessories (see pages 98 and 109).

Other Merchants

Garments and accessories of other materials were usually prepared and sold by specialist craftspeople and vendors. Leather and fur were essential materials of fashionable dress, the former used primarily for shoes and the latter to line and sometimes adorn clothing (see page 209). Leather-dressers prepared skins either by tawing with alum, tanning with oak bark or curing with lime or barley.[19] Skinners and furriers imported expensive furs such as sable and ermine for fashionable use, as well as using wild native British furs such as marten and fox. According to contemporary trade manuals, such merchants dealt with 'Skins of all Kinds that are dressed with the Hair or Fur [which are] used chiefly for lining or ornamenting Garments and Robes'.[20] Hats of plaited straw were made in Luton and imported from Italy and Bermuda. These were sold with other straw work and basketry objects, such as floor coverings, platters, chair seats, brushes and brooms, as the trade card for a 'Hat and Floor-Cloth Ware-House' illustrates.

Customers also bought the trimmings – ribbons, fringes, lace, tassels and buttons – for garments, and their arrangement was crucial in ensuring they were fashionable. The swatches of materials recording the fabrics and fringes that Barbara Johnson, a fashionable woman, purchased for her gowns in the 1760s show careful choices and matching of colour, texture and design (below). The most luxurious trimmings were sold by different types of lace-men. Some sold needle and bobbin laces, sourced from the English lacemaking counties, as well as those imported from the Low Countries and France. These lace-men required about £1,000 for their stock, 'and those, who deal in foreign Lace, may employ £10,000 to great advantage'.[21] There were other lace-men 'who by their fortunes are in the first class of tradesmen, keep very handsome shops, in which they sell all sorts of gold and silver Lace, gold and silver buttons, shapes for waistcoats, fringes, spangles, gold and silver thread, purl, twist, etc'.[22] Such an expensive and extensive stock required a 'well lin'd Pocket to Furnish his Shop' or up to £10,000 to establish a business.[23]

Trimmings made of precious metals involved a range of craftspeople. Button-makers worked silver and silver-gilt strip and threads over button moulds (see pages 198 and 200). A 'fancy and genius for inventing new Fashions, a Good Eye', and a 'clean dry Hand' were essential.[24] They sometimes also made 'frogs' (decorative knots) and tassels, although the production of these was often a specialized women's craft.[25] Because of the expense of the precious metals, lace-men usually oversaw the production of their stock, including the intricate preparation of the metal threads. Wire-drawers produced the wire of precious metals for purl and spangles (opposite, above right), and 'flatters' compressed it into the thin strips that were used in embroidery. Spinners wound the flattened strips around silk or linen thread to make silver and silver-gilt threads for weaving, needlework, buttons, tassels and fringes.[26] Buttons and trimmings made of silk and wool, such as ribbons and fringes, were supplied by haberdashers.

Makers of Clothes

Once furnished with the fabrics and trimmings of their choice, eighteenth-century customers took these to specialist makers to have them sewn into a fashionable ensemble. A seamstress or milliner made linen shirts, smocks, caps, stocks and kerchiefs; the milliner also sold these items ready-made (see page 13, above right). Tailors made men's suits, as well as individual coats, waistcoats and breeches, informal gowns and greatcoats, in addition to women's riding habits (see opposite, above left). A fashionable man relied on a tailor not only for his skill in cutting and fitting, but also for his knowledge of the latest styles, as described in *The London Tradesman*:

> His fancy must always be upon the Wing, and his Wit not a Wool-gathering, but a Fashion-hunting; he must be a perfect Proteus, change Shapes as often as the Moon, and still find something new: He ought to have a quick Eye to steal the Cut of a Sleeve, the Pattern of a Flap, or the Shape of a good Trimming, at a Glance; any Bungler may cut out a Shape, when he has a Pattern before him; but a good Workman takes it by his Eye in the passing of a Chariot, or in the Space between the Door and a Coach.[27]

The garments on pages 66 and 67 illustrate the evolution in the shape and size of men's cuffs during the eighteenth century and the subtle development a sharp-eyed tailor was expected to observe. In addition to being up to date on the latest fashions, a good tailor had to adapt them to 'bestow a good Shape where Nature has not designed it; the Hump-back, the Wry-shoulder, must be

TOP Trade card of Schneider, Skinner & Furrier, c. 1725–50

ABOVE Trade card of William Lawrence, Hat and Floor-Cloth Ware-House E.2371–1987

BELOW Fabrics and trimmings for Barbara Johnson's gowns, 1760–77 T.219–1970

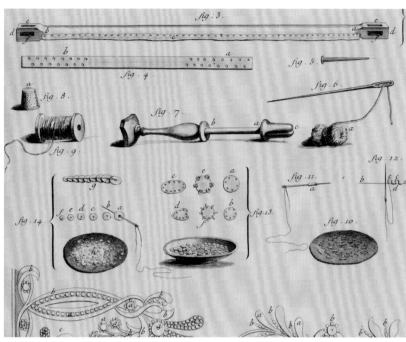

ABOVE Trade card of Benjamin Fell, Tailor, c. 1750–70

ABOVE RIGHT Varieties of metal spangles, foils and threads, Charles-Germain de Saint-Aubin, *L'Art du brodeur* (1770), plate 3

BELOW Trade card of Jonathan Nuttull, Stay-Maker, c. 1700–40

buried in Flannel and Wadding'.[28] It was not enough for a suit to look elegant when the wearer stood still; it had to move gracefully and 'sit easy in spite of a stiff Gait, or awk-[w]ard Air'.[29]

The tailor's shop included a foreman, who measured the customers, cut the fabric and finished the work, and the journeymen who sewed the seams and buttonholes.[30] In contrast to the textile suppliers, a tailor required more training but less money to establish a business: between £200 and £300 (although those making court dress might need 'as many thousands').[31] There were specialized branches of tailoring, such as robemakers, who made clerical, legal and livery gowns and parliamentary and coronation robes.[32] Stay-making was an essential craft (left), producing the garments that formed the foundation of all women's dress. This required the skill of working with whalebone (baleen), as well as 'the power of keeping secret those defects which it is frequently his [the tailor's] business to conceal, by bolstering a fallen hip, or distorted shoulder'.[33] The production of hoop petticoats (see page 84, below) was originally the work of stay-makers, but by the middle of the eighteenth century, it was a separate craft mainly practised by women. One author observed that 'the Work is harder than most Needle-work, and requires Girls of Strength. A Mistress must have a pretty kind of Genius to make them sit well and adjust them to the reigning Mode'.[34]

With the exception of riding habits, the mantua-maker made women's clothes, including court mantuas, fashionable variations of sacks, gowns, and their accompanying petticoats. A mantua-maker was considered a 'Sister to the Taylor, and like him, must be a perfect Connoisseur in Dress and Fashion'.[35] Her skills included 'a clever Knack for cutting out and fitting', and she had to 'flatter all Complexions' and 'praise all Shapes'.[36]

Fashionable accessories were made by specialist craftspeople. Shoemaking was a vast industry in the eighteenth century and one already divided into a form of 'assembly-line' production.[37] Leather-cutters cut the hides or other materials into soles and uppers of various sizes. Lastmakers carved wooden lasts in various styles and sizes for the shoemaker's use, as well as wooden heels for men's and women's shoes. The shoemaker bought these materials and made them into the finished article, often specializing in boots or men's or women's shoes.[38] Pattenmakers made wooden clogs and pattens, or overshoes, for fashionable footwear (see page 86). Shoes were sometimes made bespoke in eighteenth-century Britain, but most were sold ready-made in an established system of shoe sizing.[39]

Decoration

Embroidery was a skilled craft, indispensable in eighteenth-century fashion. Traditionally, it was executed after the tailor or mantua-maker had drawn out on the fabric the pattern pieces for a gown or suit. The embroiderers set the fabric into a frame and worked the design within the outlines of each piece (above). The fabric was then returned to the mantua-maker or tailor, who cut out the embroidered pattern pieces and sewed them together. Court mantuas (see pages 41 and 116) continued to be decorated in this way, as did other styles of women's dress (see page 133). A primary step in the evolution of 'ready-made' clothing in the eighteenth century was the development of the embroidered waistcoat 'shape' – a variation of the woven shape (see page 74, and above). The embroidered edges, pockets and buttons of a man's waistcoat or complete suit were worked on a length of silk (see pages 75, below, 127 and 202). These were sold by mercers and lace-men in the same manner as woven silks.[40] Costumers would purchase the embroidered shape they desired and take it to their tailor, who cut it out to fit, piecing the unworked parts of the silk on the sides of the waistcoat and adding a back and lining of a plain fabric. Painted silks were also decorated 'to shape' (see pages 160, 165 and 167). In contrast, decorative silks imported from China were embroidered or painted over the whole length of fabric. These were sold by mercers and drapers and, once purchased, could be made into any style of garment. Embroidered calico and chintz from India was decorated and sold in the same way.

Quilting became a specialized trade during the eighteenth century, producing gowns, banyans, petticoats and bedgowns, and waistcoats for men and women (see pages 91 and 93). The trade card (opposite, above) indicates that quilted 'coats' (petticoats, see page 89) in silk, satin, calico, russel (worsted damask), calamanco and stuff were sold ready-made.[41]

Design and Style

The pattern-drawers were central to embroidery, weaving, quilting, lacemaking, and printed and painted fabrics, linking these arts to the wider realm of eighteenth-century decorative arts (opposite). Although this occupation was

Charles-Germain de Saint-Aubin, 'The Embroiderers' Workshop', from *L'Art du brodeur* (1770), plate 2, fig. 1

considered less elevated than that of the portraitist or landscape painter, pattern-drawers were described as:

> necessary Artists for Weavers, Embroiderers, (and others who work any manner of figured Needle-work) Lace makers, Callico and Linen-printers, &c. and several of them keep Shops, who sell the Patterns ready drawn, either on Paper, or on different Sorts of Linens, Dimities, &c. for Needlework, with the proper Silks and Crewels for working them.[42]

They adapted the latest designs and decorations to the distinct techniques and dimensions of textiles, such as waistcoat shapes and quilted petticoats.[43] From the sixteenth century, pattern books and single engravings disseminated the latest designs throughout Europe, increasing in number throughout the seventeenth and eighteenth centuries.[44] Pattern-drawers used such sources as inspiration for the patterns they designed, in addition to the new styles of ornaments they observed around them.

As the selection of fashionable dress in this book illustrates, the surface designs of eighteenth-century textiles – woven, embroidered, painted or printed – all mirror the evolution of art and design of the period. Not only did they conform to contemporary styles, but the arrangement of applied decoration and the silhouette of the dressed figure also reflected the aesthetics of Baroque, Rococo and Neoclassical design. These 'style labels' were not used in the eighteenth century; they are terms devised later by art historians writing about this period. However, they are still employed to describe the stylistic characteristics of architecture, sculpture and painting of the period, as well as furniture, metalwork and ceramics, and can be usefully applied to textiles and fashion.

In the eighteenth century, the Baroque was known as the 'Italian style', because it had developed there first in the mid-sixteenth century, gradually spreading to the rest of Europe, where local and national variations evolved. The Baroque incorporated large motifs – usually foliage – rendered in curving shapes and arranged in dense patterns, giving an overall effect of movement and depth.

The Baroque colour palette favoured dark, rich shades; these characteristics can be seen in the embroidered waistcoat on page 118. Fashionable lace of the early part of the century was densely patterned with large overlapping motifs (see pages 101 and 103) filling the whole surface of the textile. The mantua was the quintessential Baroque garment, with the sculptural arrangement of the train (see page 38) echoing the carved, three-dimensional draperies characteristic of Baroque sculpture.

France was the source of the two major styles that developed in the eighteenth century: the Rococo (referred to in Britain as the 'French style') and Neoclassicism.[45] The transition between Baroque and Rococo design was a gradual one, exemplified by a lightening of palette and a reduction in the scale of motifs and their density of arrangement (see page 119). The waistcoats on page 74 epitomize the Rococo style, with the undulating rope motif creating a serpentine line on the velvet one, and the bright hues and floral motifs embellishing the embroidered shape. Not only did weavers and embroiderers embrace the Rococo, but so, too, did mantua-makers. The fashion for pinked edging (see pages 37 and 172), captures the Rococo love of asymmetry, as do the ruffles on page 171 which meander across the surface of the petticoat. Even the colours of fabrics were in harmony with other media: the bright blues, vivid greens and intense pinks of fashionable clothing of the period echo the shades of the most fashionable French porcelain (right), despite the difference in pigments and techniques required to colour ceramics and textiles. Nor were these colours associated with a wearer's gender; pink, for example, was considered an appropriate hue for a man, as the selection of men's fashions in this book demonstrates.

An entirely new aesthetic was inspired by publications illustrating the archaeological remains of Herculaneum and Pompeii, the ancient Roman cities in Italy that were excavated in the 1730s and 1740s. Although Neoclassism was everything the Rococo was not – rectilinear and geometrical in arrangement, with non-floral motifs, employing a pale and restrained palette – the transition between the two styles was very gradual in textiles and fashion. The waistcoat on page 77 retains the floral design of the Rococo, but the colours are slightly paler and the motifs smaller and arranged in a grid rather than curving lines. Designs of woven silks demonstrate a similar development (see pages 29 and 194), while lace of the 1760s and 1770s has an emphasis on a plain mesh ground, with smaller motifs (see pages 107 and 109, below). A later stage of this evolution from Rococo to Neoclassicism is evident on the waistcoat on page 153: in stark white and black, its 'flowers' are now mere abstractions represented by single spangles and beads. Perhaps the most 'classical' of the waistcoats included in this book is painted with scenes from engravings of Pompeiian wall paintings (see page 166).

In women's fashion, this transition can be seen when ruffles are no longer arranged in curves but in straight lines down the front of gown and sack skirts (see page 106), and in the decreased layering of sleeve ruffles (see pages 59–63). In the late 1790s, Neoclassicism inspired a dramatic change in the female silhouette from the wide-skirted style to a high-waisted, columnar shape (compare the diagrams on page 30 with those on page 35). In men's fashion, the eighteenth century saw a continuous reduction in silhouette, from the deep cuffs (see page 66) and full skirts (see page 19) of the Baroque decades to the narrow cuffs (see page 67, right) and very slender skirts of the Neoclassical 1790s (see page 23).

Asian Imports

The textiles of India and China had as important an impact on eighteenth-century fashion as the new styles in European art. Europe had been importing dyed and embroidered cottons from India to use as decorative furnishings since the sixteenth century.[46] Direct trade between Britain and Asia was established with the formation of the British East India Company in 1600. By the end of the seventeenth century, the Company was importing a wide range of plain and decorated Indian fabrics in a variety of textures. In order to appeal to the particular tastes of British customers, the Company sent out designs to inspire

BELOW Sèvres porcelain cup, tray and pot-pourri vase, 1757–8, French
C.456–1921, C.400–1921, C.421–1921

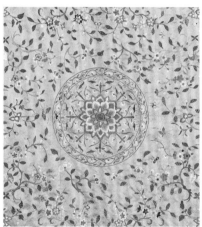

TOP Jean Pillement, title page from *A New Book of Chinese Ornaments* (London, 1755)

ABOVE Bedspread, 1770–90, of Chinese embroidered silk, c. 1770–72
T.387–1970

the Indian artists and embroiderers.[47] In turn, the unique Indian interpretations of these 'bespoke' imports influenced the designers of English silks and embroidery. By the start of the eighteenth century, this process of reciprocal exchange had been going on for several decades. The waistcoat on page 123 was clearly influenced by the embroidery technique and types of motifs decorating the petticoat on the same page, made of an Indian textile, itself following the large floral designs of seventeenth-century English crewel embroidery.[48] After the British ban on chintz was revoked in 1774, the legal import of dyed Indian textiles for fashionable dress revived (see page 158). By the end of the century, Kashmiri shawls were the latest fashion imports from India, not only worn as accessories by women but also made into men's waistcoats (see page 186, above) and inspiring the 'shawl gown' (see page 53, below).

Imports from China were also very popular in Europe; Chinese ceramics, lacquered furniture and tapestries had been available in Europe since the early seventeenth century. These prompted the production of 'chinoiserie', European objects loosely imitating Chinese styles and imagery (see the whitework apron on page 111). The naturalistic and asymmetrical qualities of Chinese art harmonized with the Rococo style, and there was a new wave of chinoiserie in the mid-eighteenth century, disseminated through books and series of prints depicting designs for lacquer, embroidery and other media (above left). China was probably the source of the popularity of yellow in eighteenth-century European fashion. It was not a shade particularly favoured in Europe in the previous century, but its importance as the colour worn exclusively by the Chinese emperor and the import of silks and wallpapers may explain the fashion for the rich yellow silks (see left and pages 79 and 171).[49] Imported Chinese embroidered and painted silks were popular, the latter inspiring English painted silks, as illustrated in chapter seven, 'Chintz and Painting'.

Absorbing all these new developments, pattern-drawers would have provided the designs for the whimsical chinoiserie boats and pavilions embroidered on the apron on page 111, the Indian-inspired flowers of the waistcoats on pages 123 and 129, the painted ones on the gown on page 165, and the classically inspired waistcoat on page 166. The garments selected for this volume reflect not only the latest in eighteenth-century design but also the individual tastes of their original owners. Just how closely a coat or gown followed the latest fashions was decided by the customer in negotiation with his tailor or her mantua-maker. Many surviving garments reveal unique combinations, such as a new style of collar with a conservatively full skirt, or the latest cut of a bodice with old-fashioned sleeve ruffles – the personal choices of their wearers. Fashion was created through the relationships between wearers, mercers, drapers, lace-men, weavers, embroiderers, tailors, milliners and mantua-makers. The garments in this book illustrate these collaborations and the variety of skills and techniques employed in eighteenth-century fashion, as well as demonstrating how it mirrored the aesthetic evolution in the decorative arts.

Notes on Captions and Descriptions

Eighteenth-century names are used to describe the garments in this book, rather than terms that have been applied to them at a later date. A different approach is taken for eighteenth-century textiles, whose terminology is complicated, specific and now either obsolete or refers to entirely different fabrics. The captions record the fibres each garment is made of, with further reference to their eighteenth-century textile names in the text. The descriptions focus on what is illustrated in the photographs and notes on alterations are only included here where they affect what is shown in the diagrams. Details about provenance – from whom an object was acquired – have been included here where available and when they shed some light on its history. More information on the garments in this volume can be found at collections.vam.ac.uk.

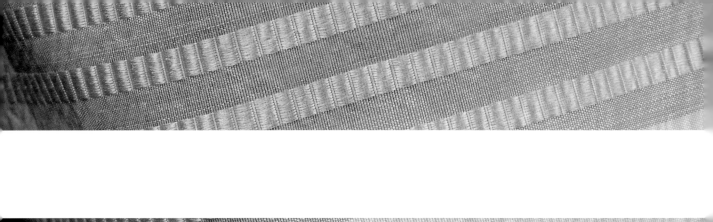

1. Pleats, Gathers and Looped Drapery

Man's silk coat
British, of French silk
1735–40
T.614:1–1996

The skirts of eighteenth-century men's coats were shaped by pleating.
In the 1730s they were very full, cut in wide curves with deep pleats
to hold them in place. As the detail illustrates, the skirts of silk coats
were usually pieced, because eighteenth-century European silks came
in narrow widths of 46–56 cm (18–22 in).

The skirts of this coat were interlined with horsehair, buckram and
a layer of unspun wool in order to hold the shape of the pleats. The side
seams are open below the hip to accommodate the wearing of a sword,
but held together at the hem with a 'stay' (a length of strong linen thread)
and a button. The coat is part of a suit with matching breeches of beige
figured silk.

Men's clothing – like women's – was subject to alteration over time;
some items of eighteenth-century men's dress in the V&A collection
were recycled for use as theatre costumes for the London stage in
the nineteenth century. Alterations to the side and back seams of this
coat and the addition of patch pockets to the linings suggest that it
might have been worn later for this purpose. This second use cannot
have been extensive, however, as the beige silk remains relatively clean.

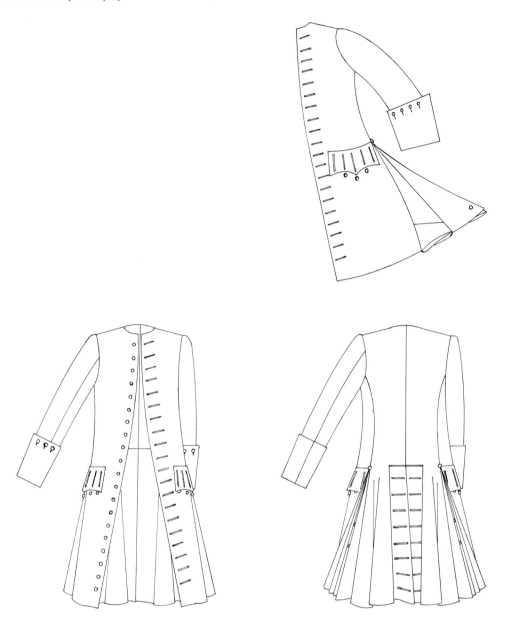

Man's wool coat
British, 1750s

T.329-1985

By the 1740s, the deep side pleats of men's coats began to decrease in volume and the side seams moved towards the centre back. Woollen broadcloth was heavily fulled so that it did not fray when cut, unlike the raw edges of silk, which had to be hemmed. On woollen suits, the raw edges of coat fronts, pockets, hems and seams were left unbound. The pleats on this example are very sharp and crisp, because there is no bulky hem at the bottom.

This coat for formal day wear has a matching waistcoat and breeches. It was an elegant, understated ensemble, with silver-gilt buttons as its only decorative highlight.

Man's silk coat
Italian, 1780s

Given by R. Brooman White, Esq.
T.147-1924

These narrow 'side' pleats – only 14 cm (5½ in) away from the centre-back edge at the hem – demonstrate how far the side seams had moved and the reduction in the volume of men's coat skirts by the 1780s. This coat has matching breeches, and the lavish silk embroidery is typical of men's court dress.

Characteristic of the 1780s is the olive-green colour of the silk, the embroidery imitating applied net, and the regular repeat of the design with sprays of flowers and leaves. Lyons was the heart of the French textile industry, producing both woven silks and embroidered ones like this example, although by the second half of the eighteenth century there were many competitors imitating Lyons silks within France and across Europe.

Several alterations were later made to this coat; it was probably worn as fancy dress in the nineteenth century. A letter from the donor's wife confirmed that her husband bought the coat in Italy in 1881.[1]

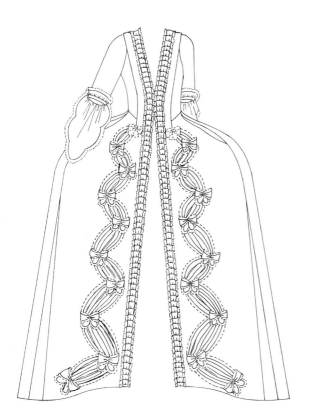

Pleats were an essential part of the construction, decoration and shape of the sack, one of the three principal styles of women's eighteenth-century dress. Known as a *robe à la française* (or simply *robe*) in France, it was called a sack, sac or sacque in Britain, or sometimes a negligée. All sacks have two (side by side) double (one on top of another) box pleats at the back. Most sacks were made of four widths of silk at the back and one width for each front. The box pleats served to adjust this width to the individual measurements of the wearer. When using a patterned silk, the mantua-maker tried to ensure the width of the pleats captured elements of the design in a symmetrical and harmonious way. Here, the top pleats highlight the floral trail of the figured silk. The fullness of the pleats, falling from shoulder to hem, created a flowing silhouette with a slight train at the back, displaying the pattern of the silk to its best advantage.

Woman's silk sack
British, 1770s

T.163–1964

The secret of fitting the same width of fabric to wearers of any size lies underneath the back pleats of a sack. While the format of two double box pleats was standard, additional material was tucked away in folds hidden beneath them. Examination of many sacks reveals that each is slightly different in the width and arrangement of the pleats underneath, varying according to the wearer's size and the pattern of the silk. This sack is made without a waist seam, which is typical of construction before the 1760s. Also characteristic of the 1750s are the very wide skirts, which would have been worn over square hoops.

The silk is a sumptuous purple, brocaded with coloured silks and a wide band of silver-gilt thread, arranged in parallel serpentine lines. Lyons, the silk-weaving centre of France, was famous for its brocades with richly coloured grounds and lavish use of metal thread.

Woman's silk sack
British, of French silk, 1755–60

T.253-1959

Silk gown

Scottish, 1775–80

Given by Miss A. Maishman
T.104-1972

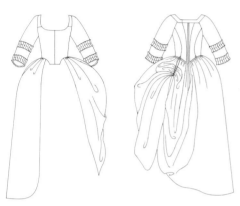

Pleats were also an essential feature of the gown, another major style of women's dress fashionable in the eighteenth century. In Britain it was called a gown, sometimes qualified as a morning or night gown, in reference to its informal status; in France, it was called a *robe à l'anglaise*. In this style, the bodice and skirt were cut in one piece only at a narrow section of the centre back. The pleats at the back of the bodice were arranged to fit the wearer and sewn in place. The skirts of the gown were pleated and stitched to the bodice around the waist.

There are two long cords sewn to the waist on the inside that attach to two buttons on the right side, looping up the skirts in the style of a polonaise. However, this is not a true polonaise, which was made without a waist seam, the bodice and skirts cut in one piece.[2] The polonaise originated in France in the 1770s and spread to Britain through fashion plates. Its unique construction was not always clear in the illustrations, and a British mantua-maker could easily have interpreted this new style as a gown with its skirts looped up (see the polonaise and fashion plate on page 44).

The donor identified this gown and those given with it (see pages 54, above and 65) as Scottish.

The wedge-shaped pleats shown here illustrate how the fullness of a sack was neatly arranged over the corners of a square hoop. By the 1770s the silhouette of the petticoat had evolved into a round shape for all but the most formal styles; a wide hoop was still required for court and evening dress. The almost square shape of the hoop that would have been worn under this example was a typically British style. This sack was made of seven widths of satin to accommodate the width of the hoop.

The ensemble was described as a wedding dress when acquired in 1947, although its formal style was more likely to have been worn for the bride's first presentation at court. In eighteenth-century Britain, elite weddings were typically held before noon and etiquette required morning dress to be worn.

Woman's silk sack
British, 1775–80

T.2-1947

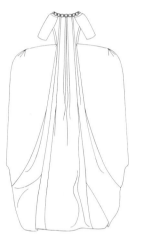

Woman's silk gown
British, 1795-9

Given by Miss Hermione Field
T.116–1938

Despite the radical changes in women's fashion in the 1790s, back pleating remained a convenient method of fitting a gown to the wearer while providing fullness to the skirt. This gown demonstrates how the traditional construction techniques of the gown (see page 28) were adapted to the new high-waisted, Neoclassical style. The arrangement of the narrow pleats on either side of the centre back is as decorative as it is structural. Three widths of silk form the skirt and back of the bodice, so the centre back is not a seam, but a small tuck with a narrow length of whalebone on either side.

The silk of this gown also reflects changing fashions in textile design. The figured satin ground is brocaded with tiny yellow leaves and small sprigs of pink and red flowers. The pale colours, simple shapes of the motifs and reduced scale of the design reveal the influence of the Neoclassical style.

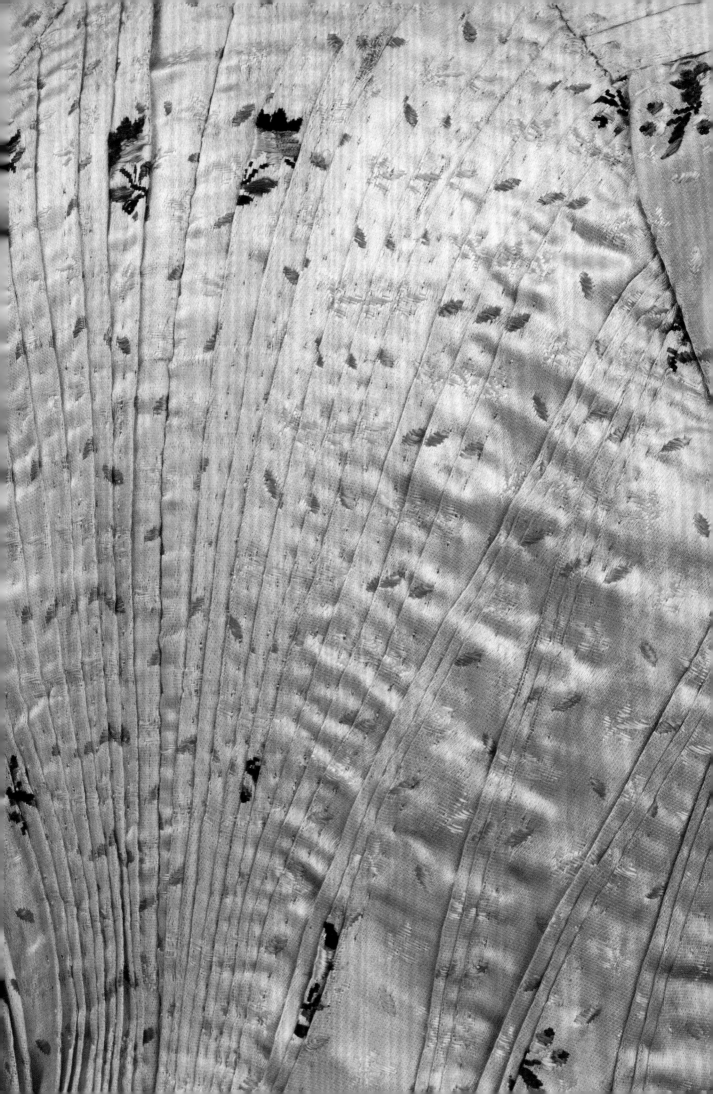

Woman's silk brunswick
French, 1765–75

T.331-1985

Pleating was an effective way of controlling the fullness of the hood on this silk brunswick. A shorter version of the sack, the brunswick usually had a hood as well as a stomacher that fastened at the front with buttons. An extension to the sleeve to cover the forearm was also typical. Those that were part of this brunswick are now lost; however, the three buttons at the elbow on the inside of each sleeve show where they would have been attached. Although the hood and longer sleeves suggest a protective outdoor garment, the watered silk used to make this brunswick was not practical, as even the lightest rainfall would have destroyed its decorative texture.

Woman's linen dressing jacket
British, 1740–80

T.28-1969

The sleeves of this linen dressing jacket are arranged in tight narrow pleats, the result of its original eighteenth-century laundering. Small stitch marks and remnants of threads suggest that the pleats were first stitched, possibly over lengths of fine straw, starched and ironed; then the straw and stitching was removed. Similar pleating can be seen on the sleeves of women's shifts and men's shirts, giving them a degree of elasticity so that they fitted comfortably under coat and gown sleeves, which became tighter after the 1740s.

The jacket is hip-length with three-quarter-length sleeves. It is made of fine Holland linen and edged around the neck and cuffs with sheer cambric frills. Women wore loose, informal jackets, made of a variety of fabrics, in the morning before dressing for the day. Linen versions, which could be washed, provided protection from the hair powder used to create fashionable hairstyles.

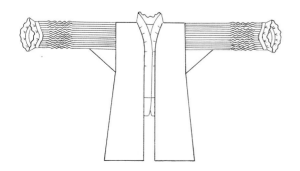

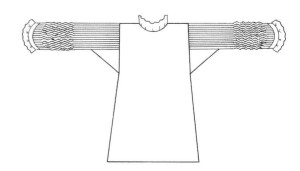

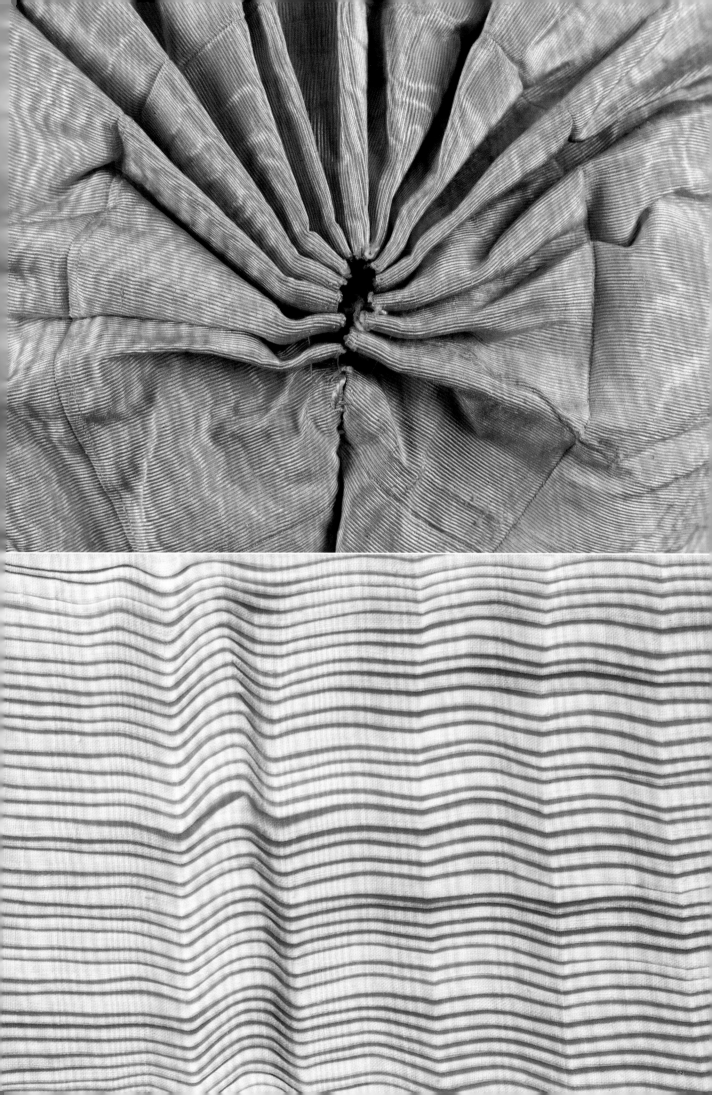

Man's wool breeches
Scottish, 1740s

Given by Sir Charles Hope Dunbar, Bt
T.250:B–1934

In the construction of men's suits, gathering was usually used only on the breeches. The seat of each leg was cut very full and gathered slightly into the back yoke. Throughout the eighteenth century most men's breeches, including those made of expensive silk brocades or velvets for court and formal wear, were cut in the same shape as breeches for riding. The latter had wide-set legs, voluminous seats and high waistbands at the back, to accommodate the positions of the torso and legs when seated on a horse.

These breeches are part of a formal day suit with a matching green woollen coat and contrasting waistcoat in a red broadcloth, all trimmed with the same silver-gilt woven lace. The suit belonged to a Scottish ancestor of the donor.

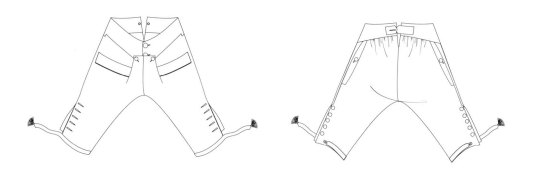

Gathers were used for construction purposes on women's dress, drawing the fullness of the sleeve ruffles into the close-fitting, elbow-length sleeves of sacks, gowns and mantuas. From the 1750s to the 1770s, the fashionable sleeve was embellished with as many as three ruffles at the elbow. The straight upper edge of the ruffle was gathered, leaving the deep scallops to curve out below. On this gown, the gathering enhances the complexity of the striped silk, with its multiple shades of pink and textured cream silk.

Woman's silk gown
British, 1770s

760–1899

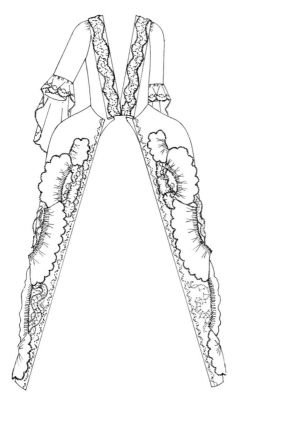

Woman's silk sack
British, 1760–65

T.426-1990

Gathering was used mainly for decorative purposes in the construction of eighteenth-century women's dress until the late 1790s. On this sack, a long strip of silk about 10 cm (4 in) wide has been tightly gathered along one edge to create a deep ruffle. It is arranged in a serpentine line and the ruffles alternate on each side of the strip as it curves. Pinking and scalloping on both sides enhance the decorative effect, and there are additional trimmings in the form of a white silk fringe and narrower bands of pinked, scalloped silk. Their curvilinear arrangement is typical of Rococo decoration and can be seen in the decoration of women's dress of the 1750s and 1760s.

The quality of the figured silk and style of decoration suggest that the sack was fashionable day wear. Its deep yellow colour was particularly popular in the eighteenth century, probably influenced by imported Chinese textiles and wallpapers (see pages 15 and 123).

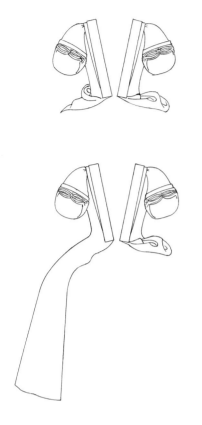

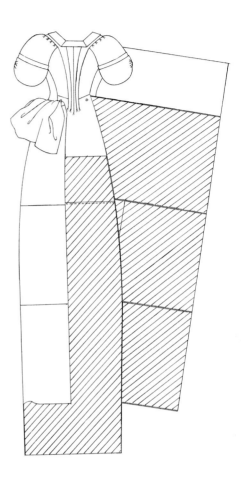

Draping was used in the early eighteenth century to create the distinctive shape of the third major garment in a woman's wardrobe, the mantua. It was open at the front with a fitted bodice and a long train draped at the back, worn over a petticoat. In the 1730s, the mantua became official English court dress and elaborate versions were worn at court throughout the eighteenth century. Mantuas in less luxurious fabrics, like this piece here, continued to be worn as formal day wear until the 1740s. They were subsequently replaced by the fashionable new style, the sack.

The mantua train required an unusual construction, joining the wrong side of one part of it to the right side of another. The diagram above shows the back view of the mantua, with one side draped and the other opened out flat, revealing how the right and the wrong sides (shaded areas) of the silk were joined. When draped and pinned in place, only the right side could be seen. Arranging the train or 'tail' successfully was a skill required of a lady's maid, and it would have been carried out every time the mantua was put on. In 1734 the Duchess of Queensbury wrote of her own mantua: 'I can assure you my tail makes a notable appearance.'[3]

Woman's silk mantua
British, 1733/4

Given by Gladys Windsor Fry
T.324-1985

Woman's silk mantua and petticoat
English, 1740–45

Given by Lord and Lady Cowdray
T.227&A-1970

The mantua, with its train and elaborate drapery, also served as court dress in Britain from the 1730s onwards, as demonstrated by this ensemble of red silk, richly embroidered with silver filé and frisé threads, strip, purl and spangles. These have been couched to the silk in an intricate 'tree of life' design, covering the petticoat and almost every surface of the mantua.

The design and execution of the embroidery is as remarkable as the signature on the wrong side of the mantua train: 'Rec'd of Mdme Leconte by me Magd. Giles'. Mme Leconte has been identified as a Huguenot embroiderer working in London between 1710 and 1746. The signature may acknowledge the full use of the 10 pounds in weight of silver thread that Mme Leconte would have received to embroider this mantua.[4] Her Huguenot connection probably explains the heavy, ornate nature of the embroidery design, which is typical of French Rococo style.

In the 1920s Lady Cowdray bought the mantua and petticoat from the fashionable London couturier Reville and had it altered to wear as fancy dress.[5]

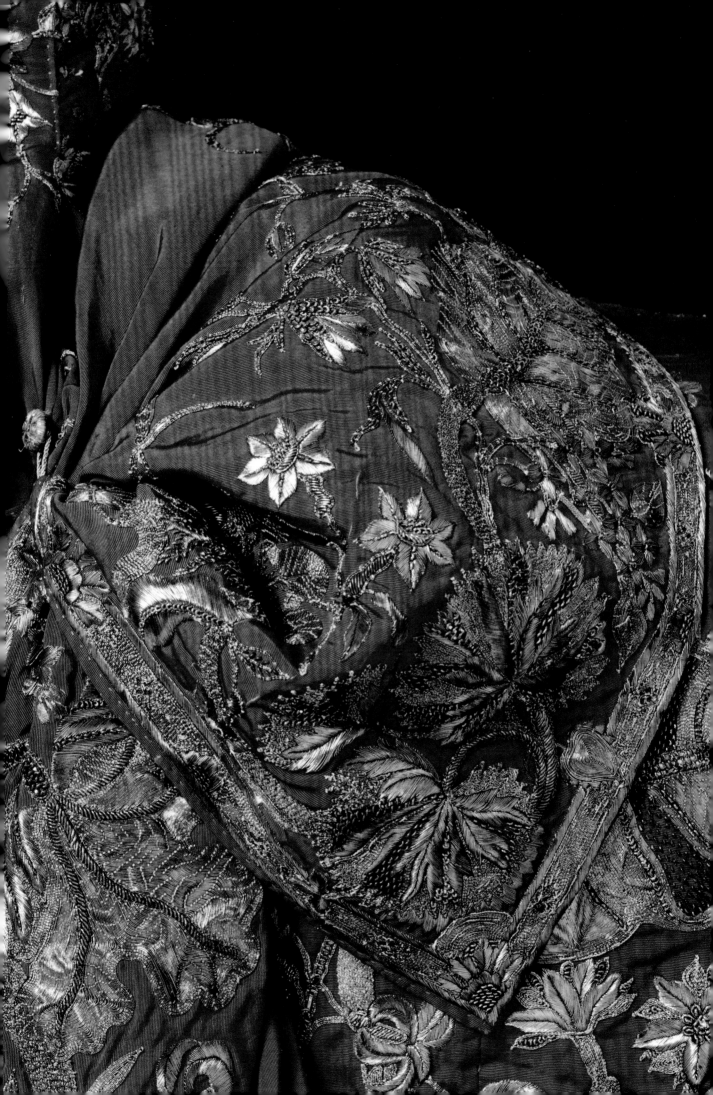

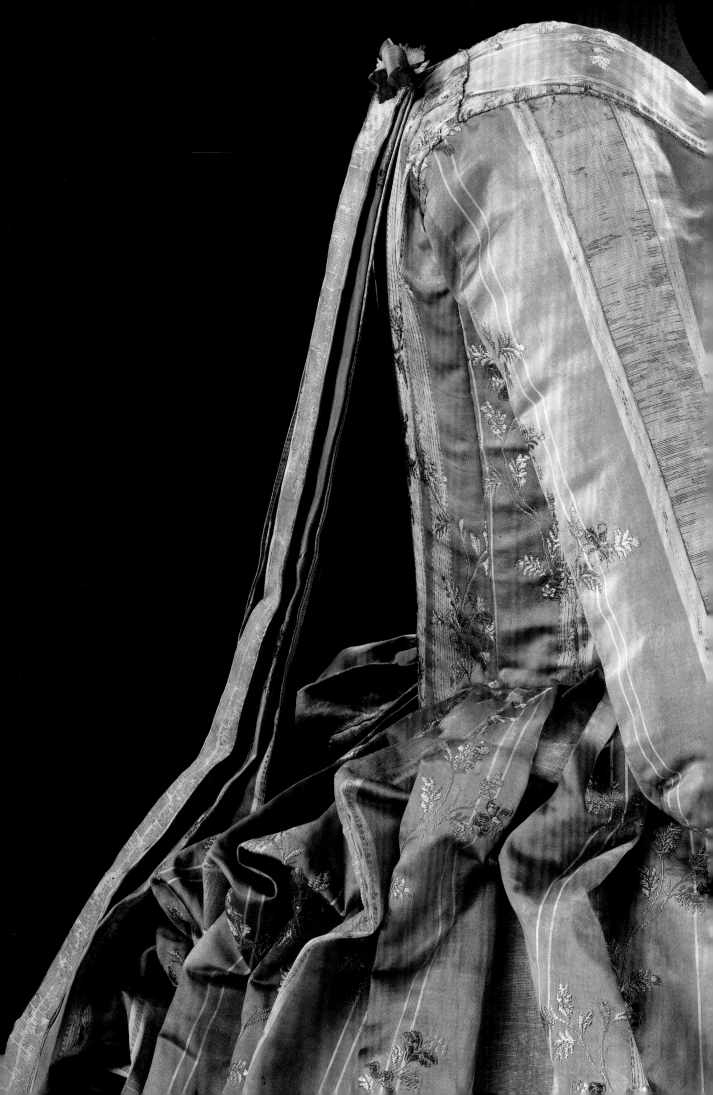

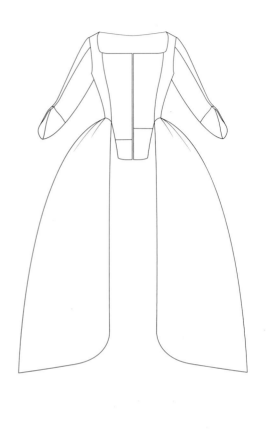

A variation of the sack known as a *robe à la piémontaise* evolved in France in the late 1770s, with the pleats at the back, separate from the bodice above the waist.[6] There are few contemporary descriptions of this short-lived style, but a plate in the French fashion series *Gallerie des modes et des costumes français* (published between 1778 and 1787), is labelled *piédmontese*. (Although the separate pleats cannot be seen in the illustration, shown right, the description accompanying the plate notes that they are separate, attaching at the back of the neck.) According to the *Gallerie*, the style was first worn by Clotilde of France, Princess of Piedmont, to the theatre in Lyons in 1775.[7]

Inside the skirt is a semicircle of metal rings. When these are threaded through with a tape and pulled up, the pleats stand out, creating a distinctive silhouette. This draping can also be seen on surviving *robes à la française*, for example in the Musée de la Mode et du Costume in Paris.[8]

This piedmontese has a matching petticoat, and both are made of satin, with stripes of white satin embroidered with silver-gilt thread and tawny satin brocaded with trails of flowers and leaves. It was probably made first as a *robe à la française*, then the back pleats detached and bodice adjusted to create the piedmontese style about 1780. The petticoat was altered in the late nineteenth century when the ensemble was worn as fancy dress.

Woman's silk piedmontese
French, 1775–80

750&A-1898

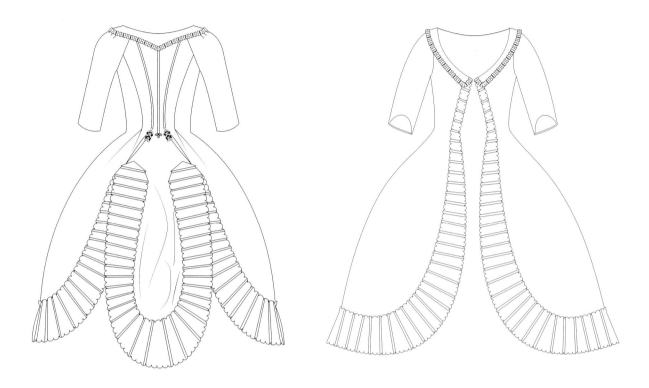

Woman's silk polonaise
British or French, 1775–80

Presented by Miss Eva Mahon and Miss
Constance Mahon of Bournemouth through
the National Art Collections Fund
T.20–1945

Draped skirts were a distinctive characteristic of another French
fashion of the 1770s: the polonaise. In 1778 several examples of this new
style were illustrated in the series of fashion plates *Gallerie des modes
et des costumes français* (see left).[9] Recent scholarship has revealed that
many so-called polonaises were in fact English gowns with looped up
skirts (see page 28).[9] A true polonaise was cut in four pieces: two backs
and two fronts, with no waist seam. It opened at the front, with the
edges cut to fall away in an inverted 'V' shape, which was filled in with
a 'false waistcoat' or an inverted stomacher. Unlike any earlier styles
of eighteenth-century gown, the polonaise had a narrow collar.

This 'true' polonaise, the only example in the V&A collection, is
missing both its petticoat and stomacher, as well as one of the chain-
looped lengths of silk gimp used to loop up the skirts. In the nineteenth
century it was worn as fancy dress, and darts (now unpicked) were
sewn into the bodice fronts.

Man's silk coat
British, 1750s, of French or English silk

Given by Miss Agnes Clayton East
T.137–1932

At the beginning of the eighteenth century, men's coats had no collars, only a narrow binding of fabric around the neck, as seen in this example. Formal coats and those for court remained collarless well into the 1760s, although a small turn-down collar appeared on the informal coat known as a 'frock' in the 1730s (see page 68).

This coat is part of a suit, with matching waistcoat and breeches. The design of the silk, with diagonal scrolls and small floral motifs in cerise and cream, is typical in palette and scale of the fabrics used in men's clothing in the mid-eighteenth century, and it could have been woven in England or France. Such a luxurious silk would have been worn for formal evening occasions such as going to the theatre or the opera. The lack of additional decoration suggests that the suit was made and worn in Britain, where taste in masculine dress was more restrained than in France.

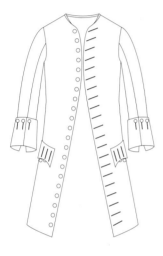
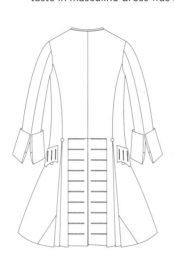

Man's silk coat
French or English, 1760–65

Given by Messrs Harrods
T.707–1913

A small collar had become part of men's formal coats by the early 1760s, a narrow, stand-up version replacing the earlier neck binding. This coat has matching breeches of figured silk, now quite faded but once a subtle medley of carnation pink and three shades of silvery grey. The ensemble was part of a large collection of historical dress owned by Talbot Hughes. Hughes was an artist specializing in allegorical and historical scenes (very popular genres in the late nineteenth century), for which he collected eighteenth- and early nineteenth-century fashions from second-hand markets. When he put the collection up for sale in 1913, he was offered $5,000 by an American department store, who intended to give it to the Metropolitan Museum of Art in New York. Instead, the collection was bought by Harrods, in London, and donated to the V&A.

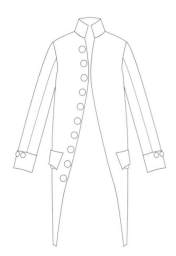
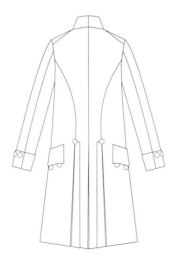

Man's silk coat
British, 1785–90

Given by Phoebe Timpson
T.363–1995

By the late 1780s, fashionable collars were much higher and turned down, with a point at the centre back, as seen on this coat of salmon-pink ribbed silk. The coat is plain except for a woven lace of ivory- and yellow-striped grosgrain with silver strip and thread, and matching buttons. The light palette and simple decoration illustrate the move away from the bright colours and more elaborate Rococo style of previous decades. For a detail of this coat's buttons, see page 202, right.

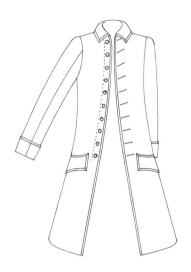
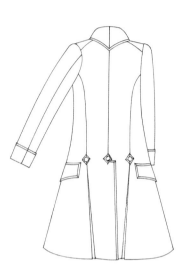

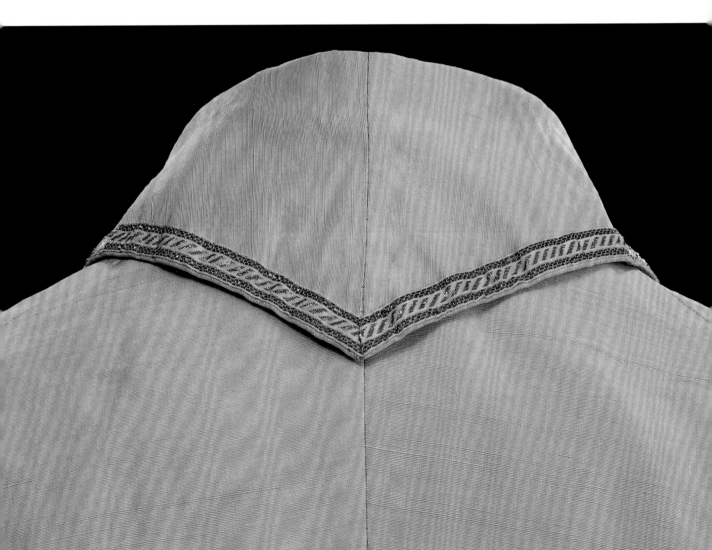

The collar continued to grow in height, reaching its apogee in the late 1790s, and coat fronts turned back into wide revers. Although made of a very lightweight silk, these revers have no interlining, only a facing of the same silk. The collar is cut in two pieces; the stand-up part has a light interlining and is lined with silk, while the turn-down part is a single layer of the green silk. Both are tacked together at the top front to hold the collar upright. The vivid green silk, high waist, and buttons without corresponding buttonholes are typical of the more flamboyant styles of men's Neoclassical dress.

Man's silk coat
French, 1790s

Given by Messrs Harrods
T.731–1913

Woman's wool riding coat
British, 1750s

T.198-1984

Until the advent of the polonaise in the 1770s (see page 45) there were no collars on any style of women's gown. They were, however, a feature of women's riding coats, which were made by tailors in the style of men's coats. In this example, careful arrangement of the seams makes a virtue of the piecing of the collar's silk. The same silk faces the cuffs and lines the pocket flaps, contrasting with the crisp worsted fabric of the coat.

Other elements of the masculine coat, such as long sleeves, buttoned fronts and pockets, are found on eighteenth-century women's riding habits. A waist seam and sometimes a small dart at the front edges – both necessary for a smooth fit over a pair of stays – distinguish a woman's version of this garment from a man's coat.

Woman's silk and wool gown
British, 1795–1800

T.217-1968

In the late 1790s collars appeared more frequently on women's dress, particularly informal styles. In this example the simple, one-layer, two-piece collar is typical in shape and construction. During this decade it was fashionable to wear shawls imported from Kashmir as accessories, as well as to make them into gowns. The shawl here is unlike most European ones of this period, which were woven in patterns imitating the Kashmiri imports; it is block-printed on a silk weft and wool warp, and its design echoes the blurred effect of European chiné silks. The Leven Printfields in Dunbartonshire, Scotland, were one of the earliest manufacturers of printed shawls, and this may be one of theirs.[1] The shawl was cut in half across the centre and the two pieces sewn together lengthwise, with the border at the hem. The use of a short sleeve over a wrist-length one recalls the similar arrangements used on the *robe à la turque* and *robe à la circassienne*, both fashionable in the 1770s and 1780s.[2]

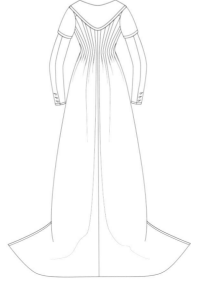

Woman's silk gown
Scottish, 1795–9

Given by Miss A. Maishman
T.95–1972

The only black gown in the V&A collection, the plain, slightly dull texture of the silk and lack of any adornment identify this gown as an early example of mourning dress. The deep collar at the back is a single layer of silk, and horizontal fold marks suggest that it was worn softly pleated. It continues over the shoulders into the bodice fronts, which were caught under the bust with a narrow tie. Piecing and stitch marks indicate that the gown was made from something else, and the panel missing from the left front (indicated in the diagram by the dotted lines) suggests that it was in the process of being recycled again. The donor identified the gown and those acquired with it (see pages 28 and 65) as Scottish.

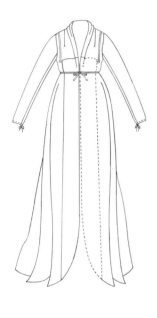 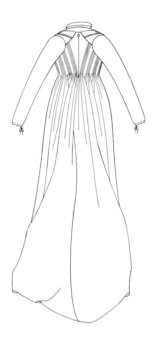

Woman's muslin gown
British, 1795–9

T.104–1968

This gown illustrates how the collar at the back continued over the shoulders to form the bodice fronts, a style typical in the late 1790s. In contrast to the gown shown above, the collar here is closely pleated and stitched at the centre back. Diagonal pleating shapes the back of the bodice and adds texture to the sleeves of the gown, which is made of plain white muslin and decorated with glued silver spots.

Woman's silk mantua
British, 1735–40

T.9-1971

A deep, close-fitting cuff shaped with narrow pleats at the front was the typical style for mantuas and gowns in the 1730s. This mantua and its matching petticoat were formal day wear, very similar in style to the ensemble seen on page 38. The silk, woven in Spitalfields, London, is characteristic of this decade, with a large-scale floral pattern brocaded with floss silk and silk chenille threads in shades of green, rust and maroon on a brown ground.

The mantua and its petticoat were purchased by the V&A from a Hampshire drama group that had been given them to use as stage costume. Fortunately, one of the group recognized the ensemble's historical significance and offered it to the V&A.

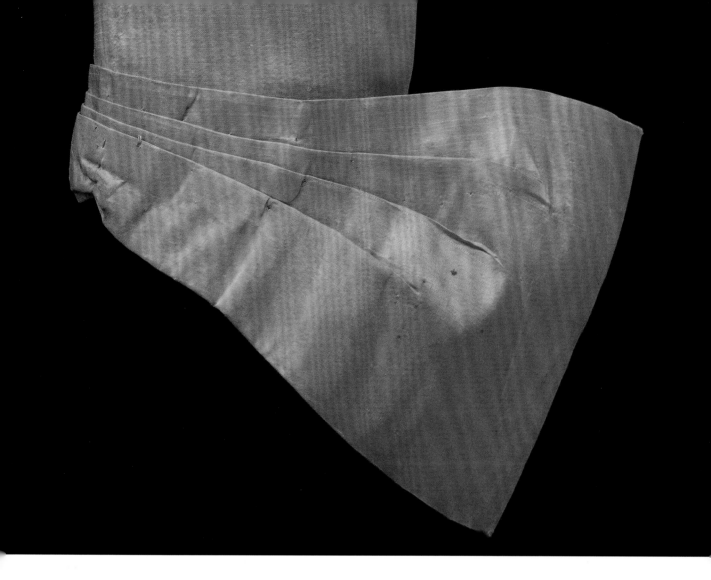

In the 1740s the cuff began to extend away from the sleeve, as this silk taffeta bodice demonstrates. The cuff is narrower in front and has fewer pleats than the one shown opposite, and its circumference is larger than that of the sleeve, creating a winged effect.

The undecorated bodice is made of eight panels of silk and laces up the centre back. Each side of the centre-back opening is boned and constructed with a fly to conceal the lacing (not shown in the drawing). Worn with a matching petticoat, this style of bodice was the typical ensemble for children and young girls, as well as informal dress for adult women. The front side seams of this bodice have been let out, piecings added to the side-back seams and triangles of silk inserted into the underarm seams to accommodate a growing girl.

Girl's silk bodice
British, 1740s

Given by the Rev. R. Brooke
870–1864

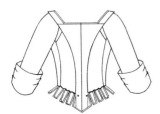

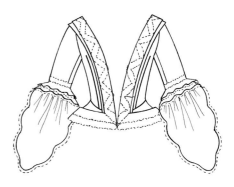

Woman's silk mantua
British, 1750s

T.44-1910

In the 1750s the wing cuff was replaced by sleeve ruffles with scalloped edges, usually worn in threes and graduating in size. On gowns, sacks and mantuas the shape and layering of sleeve ruffles exemplified the Rococo influence on the fashionable silhouette. These ruffles are part of a court mantua made of a Spitalfields brocaded silk, woven about 1745, and trimmed with coloured silk bobbin lace. Once a fresh green, warm salmon-pink and ivory, the lace has faded from exposure to light.

The drawings show that by the 1750s, the fluid drapery of the 1740s mantua (see pages 38 and 41) had been replaced by a gathered band of robing, continuing from the front of the bodice around the side and across the back at the waist. The side panels of the train still fold around to the back and they remain reversed so that the right side of the fabric shows, but they are now stitched to the waist rather than folded over a looped cord. The darts in the front bodice, shown in the drawing, are nineteenth-century modifications for fancy dress.

By the 1760s the triple sleeve ruffle was reserved for court dress, and more informal styles were adorned with only one or two, as seen on this sack. The blue silk damask is woven in an all-over pattern of large flowers and leaves. The silk dates from about 1742 and is probably English; in surviving eighteenth-century women's dress there is often a gap between the date of the fabric and that of the garment. This reflects both the parsimonious habits and conservative approach to fashion of the members of the gentry who wore these clothes, echoed in eighteenth-century moral guidance on dress: 'The best Rule here I believe is neither to be among the first to take up with a new Fashion, nor among the last to drop an old one; and neither to be remarkably dressed in the Tip Top of the Mode, nor too far below it.'[3]

Woman's silk sack
British, 1760s

Given by the Surrey County Federation of Women's Institutes
T.122–1957

Woman's silk gown
British, 1760s

Given by Mrs H. H. Fraser
T.433–1967

The weave of this silk gown uses a complex system of binding that makes its pattern of rose-red ground and trails of white flowers reversible. It was woven in the 1740s; the gown was possibly made then and altered in the following decades. The last update was in the 1760s, when the stomacher was replaced with buttoned tabs. There may have been two sleeve ruffles originally, and the upper one cut off to leave a pleated border above a single ruffle.

Many surviving silk garments have been remodelled and updated through several decades of fashionable changes. Clothing was passed to poorer relatives, friends or servants, as well as to the local church, where the expensive silks were converted into altar frontals and ecclesiastical vestments. Mrs Charlotte Papendiek, an assistant wardrobe keeper and a companion to Queen Charlotte in the 1780s and 1790s, records in her diary how she kept a puce satin gown going for seven years, repeatedly altering its decoration:

> Fashion, too, was not then exigent in the matter of continual change. A silk gown would go on for years, a little furbished up with new trimmings – and a young woman was rather complimented than otherwise when she exhibited care of her possessions, and might, with no discredit to herself, appear time after time in the same attire.[4]

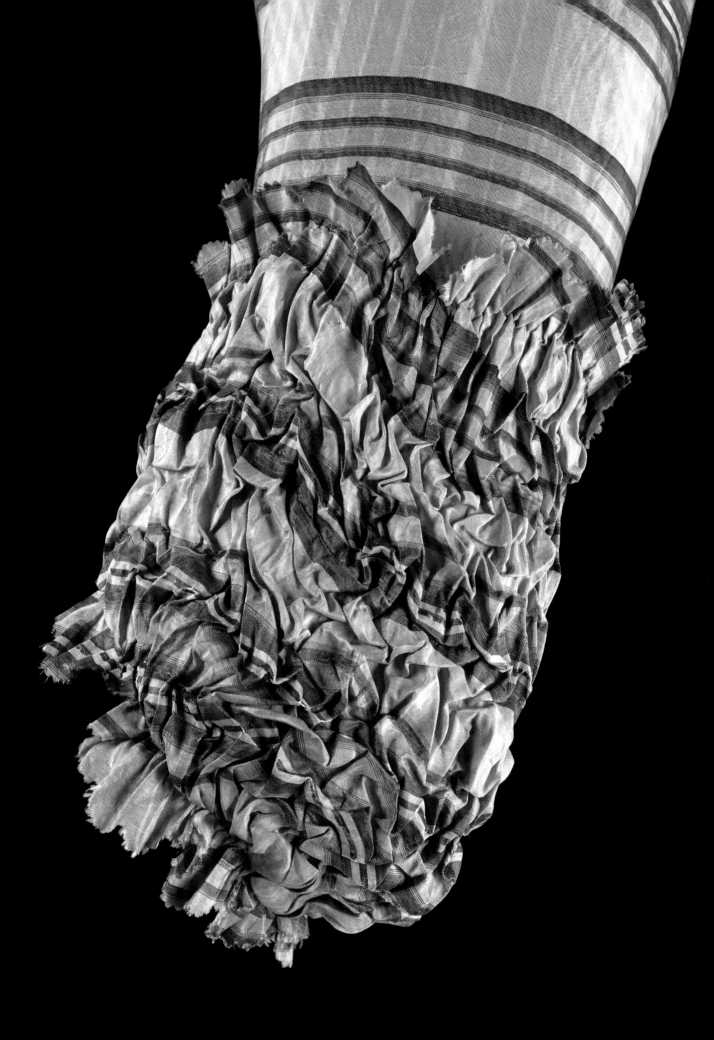

By the 1770s the sleeve ruffle had disappeared from informal gowns, replaced by a plain round or pleated cuff, or a shirred one, like this example. Stripes were popular during this decade and the complex arrangement of shaded and contrasted stripes of pink, maroon, yellow and white creates an interesting visual effect when gathered. Close inspection of this gown and its matching petticoat reveals that they have been remade from another garment, perhaps an earlier style with sleeve ruffles and front robings. The gown was unpicked and carefully pieced together using every scrap of fabric, and the new cuffs were converted from a sleeve ruffle.

The donor identified the gown and those acquired with it (see pages 28 and 54) as Scottish.

Woman's silk gown
Scottish, 1770–75

Given by Miss A. Maishman
T.92–1972

Man's silk coat
British, 1730s
658-1898

A deep, gently rounded cuff is the stylistic focus of this unadorned silk coat of the 1730s. Known as an open cuff or open sleeve, the cuff extended above the elbow, as seen in this example. Made of fawn-coloured ribbed silk, the coat is typical of English formal day wear, which usually had little or no ornament. Subdued shades of mauve, beige and grey were fashionable in the early eighteenth century.

Man's wool coat
British, 1740s
Loan from Past Pleasures Ltd

Mirroring the changes in women's dress (see page 57), this men's woollen coat of the 1740s has a slightly narrower cuff that extends away from the sleeve. More formal than the coat shown on the left, it has a matching waistcoat and breeches, and all are decorated with silver woven lace and silver buttons, cast to imitate a death's head design (see page 203, left).

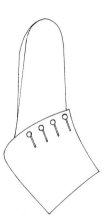

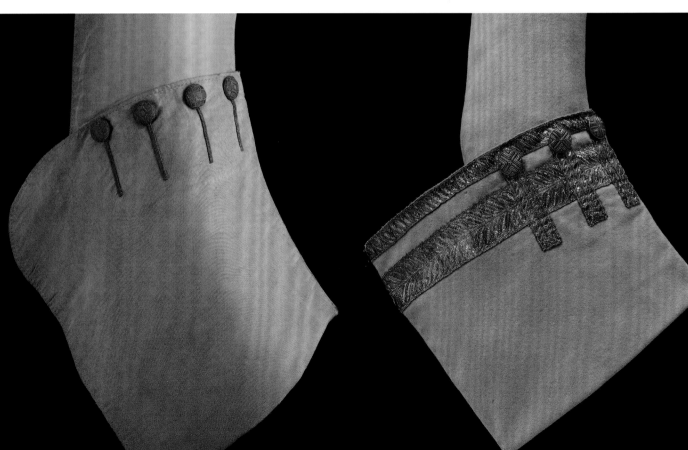

Man's silk coat
British, 1765–70, of French or English silk, 1760s

T.114–1953

By the 1760s a simple round cuff of moderate depth
had replaced the winged styles of earlier decades.
This vibrantly patterned silk tissue with a design
of flowers and meandering band of lace is typical
of French production, which was closely copied
by Spitalfields weavers.

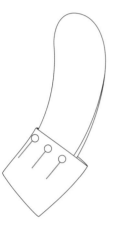

Man's silk coat
British, late 1780s

Given by Mrs N. J. Batten
CIRC.455–1962

The cuffs on the snugly fitting sleeves of this 1780s
coat are narrower and tighter than those on the left.
They have a slit with an attached flap, a non-functional
variation of the mariner's cuff (see page 68). The
iridescent blue and green changeable, ribbed silk
illustrates a move away from the patterned silks
fashionable in earlier decades.

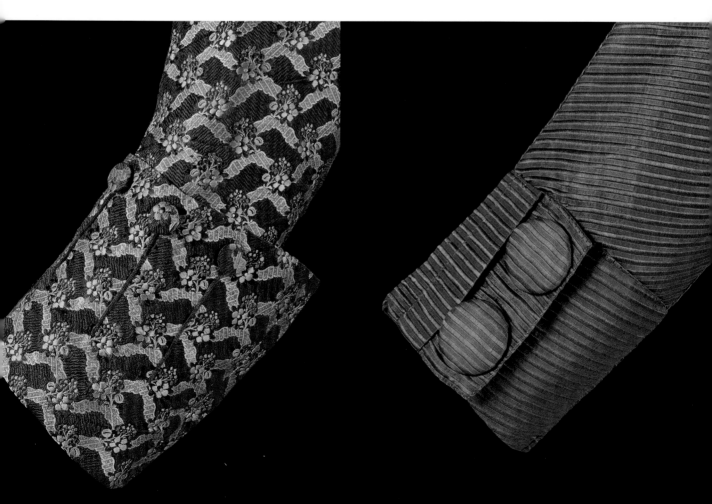

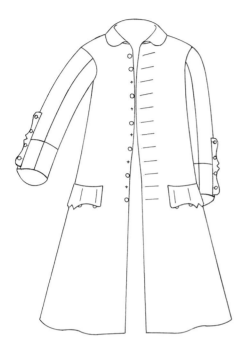
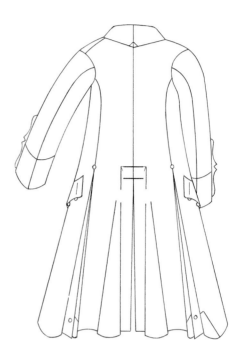

The thick woollen fabric of this strictly utilitarian coat lends a sculptural quality to the mariner's cuff of the sleeve. A vertical opening with a scalloped flap runs parallel to the length of the sleeve, intersecting with the cuff. This style of cuff became popular in the 1750s, first seen on coats worn a decade earlier by naval and military officers (naval and army uniforms were not made official until 1748 and 1751, respectively). Unlike the cuff on the previous page, the buttons on this one can be undone, allowing the sleeve to be opened. Mariner's cuffs were also popular for women's riding habits, as seen in the example on the right.

The coat's turn-down collar, seen in the drawings, identifies the coat as a man's informal frock. This new casual style of coat appears in portraits dating from the 1730s, but surviving early frocks are rare; this is the earliest example in the V&A. A label sewn to the inside collar indicates that this coat once belonged to the nineteenth-century theatrical costumiers L. & H. Nathan, where it experienced a second and more arduous life.

Man's wool coat (opposite, above)
British, 1750s

467-1907

Woman's worsted coat (below)
British, 1750s

T.197-1984

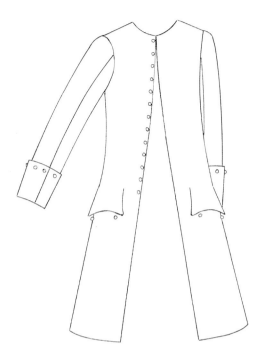 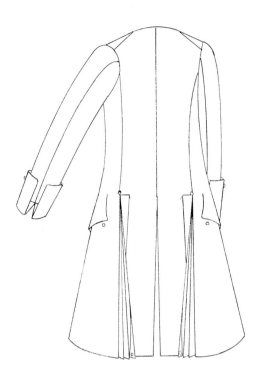

The cuffs of men's court and formal coats were often elaborately decorated with embroidery or applied woven laces. On this coat of figured silk velvet, both the cuff and its lining of white satin have been embroidered with silver-gilt purl, spangles and thread. The same decoration adorns the pockets and fronts of the coat.

The donor identified the coat and its accompanying waistcoat as having an Italian provenance.

Man's silk coat
Italian, 1760s
Given by Mr W. R. Crawshay
T.28-1952

Pockets on men's coats and waistcoats were a focus for decoration in the eighteenth century. On this waistcoat, embroidery with silver thread, foil and spangles embellishes the pocket flap and the area around it, as well as the front edges and hem. Its design epitomizes the Rococo style, with curvilinear floral elements and the motif of a winding ribbon with scalloped edges. The embroidery is worked over pieces of card or parchment to give a raised effect and sharp definition to the edges of the motifs. There is a silver passementerie button stitched to each corner of the pocket flap and four below the pocket – all purely decorative, as there are no buttonholes.

Man's silk waistcoat
British, 1740s

Given by Mrs C. C. Stisted
T.29-1950

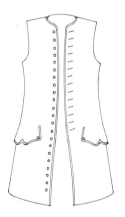
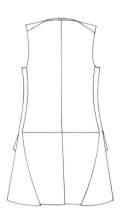

For most of the eighteenth century, the pocket flaps of men's coats and waistcoats had the characteristic three-pointed shape shown in this example. Made of superfine red broadcloth, the coat and its pocket flaps are lined with light-blue silk taffeta, which has been eased around the edges to appear like a fine line of piping. There are two functioning buttons with buttonholes, one at either end of each pocket flap, with a decorative one in the centre. The buttons are covered in red foil and embroidered with silver spangles and silver thread.

Man's wool coat
French or Dutch, 1770

T.214:1-1992

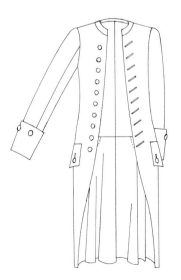
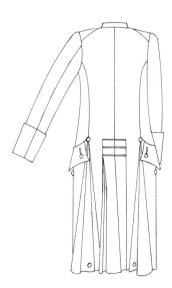

The pattern of this velvet was woven to the shape of a waistcoat; it was not meant to be used for any other type of garment. By the 1730s, French silk manufacturers had begun to weave their velvets expressly to be made into waistcoats. The pattern along the curving centre-front edges, the corners at the lower hem and on the pocket-flap shapes is woven into the fabric length, a technique called *à disposition* or 'woven to shape'. The neckline, side seams and armholes are not outlined in the woven pattern, allowing the tailor to cut them to fit the wearer.

In this snuff-coloured velvet of the 1750s, the pattern is made of cut, uncut and voided velvet in a typically Rococo design of flowers, meandering rope motif and dentellated scrolls. As splendid as the silk velvet is, the back of the waistcoat is even more exceptional, made of a rare piece of cotton velvet woven in a decorative pattern, shown right.

Man's silk waistcoat
British, of French velvet, 1750s
T.197–1975

This length of embroidered silk demonstrates the *à disposition* principle in embroidery. Two widths of ivory ribbed silk have been tamboured (chain stitch worked with a hook) in a pattern of roses, exactly to the shape of a waistcoat front piece. A tailor making this up would have used a plain silk or wool for the back and fustian for the lining. The waistcoat shape illustrates the high calibre of French tambour work, which is remarkably fine and even.

It also demonstrates the efforts to which the English went to acquire desirable French fashions. On the wrong side of the lower right edge is a stamp reading 'Custom House I SEIZED DOVER I GR II'. This is contraband, a French waistcoat shape apprehended when someone tried to smuggle it into England during the reign of George II. For most of the eighteenth century, heavy duties and sometimes outright bans were imposed on the import of French silks and laces in order to protect British textile industries. Despite this, smuggling of these and other taxable goods was endemic throughout all levels of English society. This pair of shapes might have arrived in England concealed in a false-bottomed trunk, hidden underneath a lady's hoop or stitched between two layers of a worn old nightgown.[5]

Man's waistcoat shape
French, 1750s
T.12–1981

Man's silk waistcoat

British or French, 1785–90, of French
embroidered silk, after 1784

T.200-2016

The embroidery of late eighteenth-century waistcoats often incorporated pictorial imagery, as demonstrated by this waistcoat. A balloon adorns its pockets and many more float across its front, documenting a crucial event in the history of manned flight. Each balloon is a complete globe of striped colour, with a shallow gondola (basket) and flags hanging over its sides. It corresponds very closely to the style of balloon used for the first manned hydrogen-filled balloon flight, held at the Jardin des Tuileries on 1 December 1783, by Jacques Charles, Nicolas-Louis Robert and his brother Anne-Jean, and Joseph-Michel Montgolfier.[6]

The public demonstrations of balloon flights in Europe caused great popular excitement, and images of them were widely disseminated through media such as textiles and ceramics. This waistcoat was probably embroidered in France as a 'shape', but would have been available to buy throughout Europe. It may have been made into a waistcoat in England (where the Italian aeronaut Vicenzo Lunardi demonstrated his hydrogen balloon in London in 1784). Made of silk with metal thread embroidery and in the old-fashioned, skirted style, the waistcoat was probably intended for formal wear.

This waistcoat illustrates the development in style by the end of the eighteenth century. Gone are the skirts and pocket flaps; the latter have been reduced to a border on the lower edge of the straight pocket opening, and the waistcoat ends in a straight line at the hips.

The waistcoat is decorated with tambouring, satin stitch and couched chenille thread, and the influence of Neoclassical design is evident in its palette and decoration. In comparison with the vibrant hue of the embroidery on the 1750s waistcoat shape on page 74, the pink of this 1790s example is much more subdued. The rhythmic Rococo meanders and sprays of naturalistic flowers are now straighter, more stylized and geometric, as well as smaller in scale. A zigzag between two straight lines adds a little movement, while a gentle twist of almost abstract flowers and leaves edges the front and lower hem.

Man's silk waistcoat
British, 1790s

Given by the family of Dr and Mrs Hildred Carlill
T.355-1985

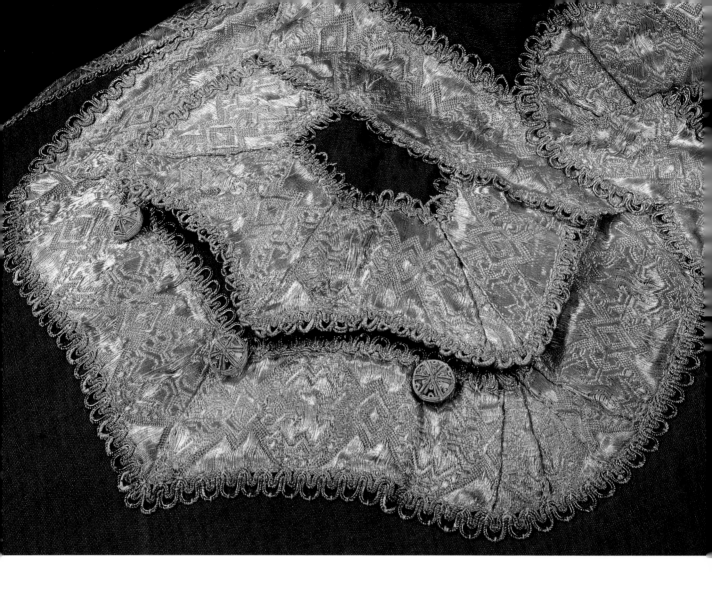

Woman's wool riding coat

British, 1750s

T.554-1993

Women's riding coats and waistcoats imitated the style and tailoring of men's garments and included pockets as part of the construction. The narrow, pointed waist and flared skirts of this worsted riding coat are typical of the 1750s, as are the Rococo curves of the braid. The wide, woven lace imitates the splendour of military braid at the same time as it accentuates the wearer's figure. It has been expertly mitred to angle the lace around the pockets, pocket flaps and cuffs, and into wide scallops around the buttons and buttonholes down the front. The trimming consists of three parts: a 4.8cm-wide (1 ⅞ in) lace of silver thread woven in a geometrical pattern, with lengths of a narrow lace (0.8cm/⅓ in) of silver gimp stitched on either side.

Except on riding coats, pockets were not sewn into women's dress in the eighteenth century but worn as a separate accessory. Single pockets or a pair were sewn to a tape that tied around the waist under a hoop and petticoat. Access to the pockets and their contents was gained through openings in the side seams of the petticoat and the gown or sack worn over it. Although unseen, pockets were frequently decorated; this pair is quilted in a diaper pattern, with a scrolling wave design around the border.

Pair of quilted silk pockets
British, 1740s

T.87:A–1978

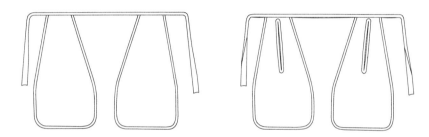

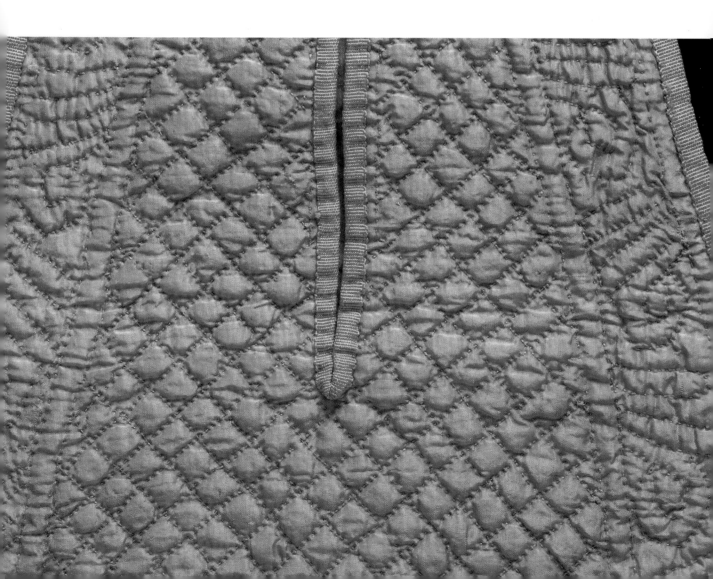

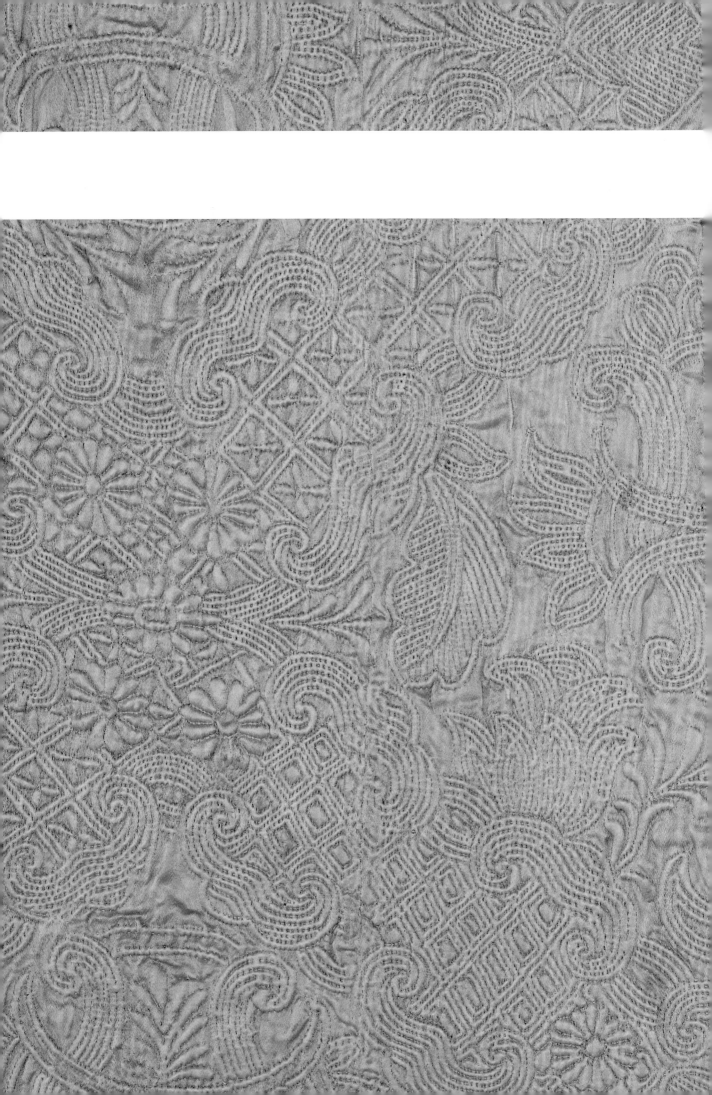

3. Stitching and Quilting

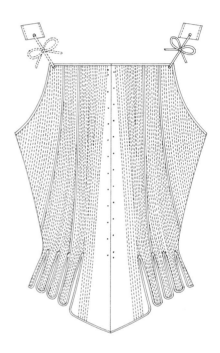

Pair of wool stays
British, 1780–90

Given by the family of Mrs Jane Robinson
T.192–1929

White stitching and silk ribbon emphasize the main seam lines and add a decorative contrast to these boned stays. Although stays were undergarments and not meant to be visible, their fine, regular stitching is a crucial part of their composition as well as their aesthetic appeal. Narrow rows of even hand-stitching form the compartments into which the thin strips of whalebone (baleen) were inserted to give the stays their rigid shape. The stitching and whalebone follow the diagonal shaping of the stays that was essential in creating the fashionable silhouette of the 1780s. These stays are made of three layers of fabric, the outer one of red wool, an inside layer probably of coarse linen (forming the other side of the whalebone compartments) and a linen lining. Women's stays were made by men and their methods of construction were part of the tailoring tradition.

Man's linen shirt
British, 1740–80

Given by Mrs H. Egland
T.246-1931

Extremely fine stitching was one of the skills required in making linen undergarments – shirts for men and shifts for women. This detail of the neck of a man's shirt reveals the very small, regular stitches and the minute gathers. The topstitching of the neck gusset and shoulder strap is a very simple form of drawn-thread work. A single thread of the linen weave was pulled out and a row of back-stitch worked in its place. Such fine sewing was essential not only for the comfort of the wearer but also to ensure that the seams held together when the linens were washed.

The production of linens, including shirts, shifts and baby clothes, as well as accessories such as caps, cuffs, cravats and kerchiefs, was traditionally a women's craft. In the eighteenth century these linens were made by seamstresses and sold by female milliners.

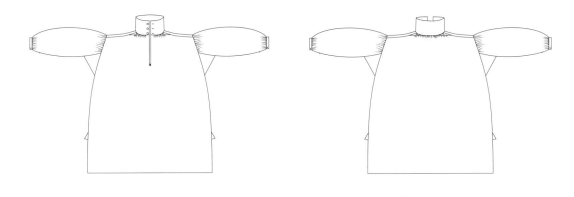

Woman's linen hoop petticoat
British, 1740s

T.425-1990

In contrast to the stays on page 83 and the shirt above, fairly coarse stitching was used on another form of women's undergarment, the hoop petticoat, demonstrating the utilitarian approach to construction of eighteenth-century makers. Coarsely woven linen, sometimes recycled from other garments, was used to make hoops. Two circles of split cane with a diagonal piece on each side create the rounded-square shape of this English-style hoop. Although the silhouette of the petticoats worn over this form of support often appears very solid and unwieldy, the hoops themselves are light in weight and shaping was needed only at the hips.

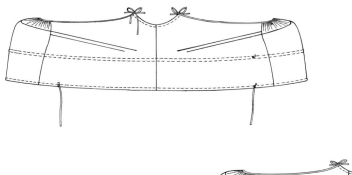

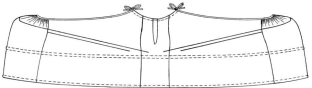

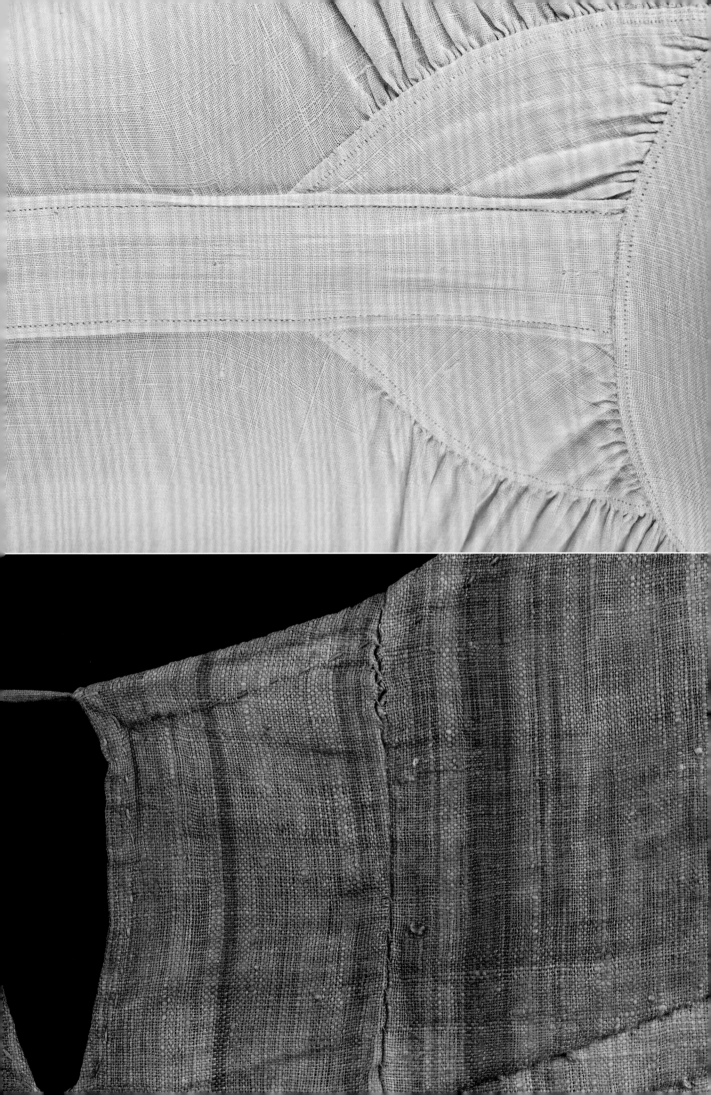

Fine, regular stitching was essential in shoemaking, in this example holding the layers of the leather sole together and joining the red leather side pieces of the instep to the sole. In shoemaking, 'stitching' refers to seams where the thread can be seen on both sides, while 'sewing' refers to those where the thread is visible only on one side. Thick, waxed hemp threads were used, with a wild boar's bristle instead of a needle; the bristle was split at one end and the thread placed inside and wrapped around. A bristle was attached to each end of the thread, and each went through a stitch hole (made with an awl) in opposite directions.[1] On the fabric upper of these pattens, a running stitch holds the silk ribbon binding to the green velvet. There is also some purely decorative stitching in the form of the spiral on the red leather sides.

Pattens, or 'galoshes', as they were often called in the eighteenth century, were worn over shoes to protect them from muddy streets. They were usually cut and made to fit over a particular pair of shoes.[2] The shoes that were worn with these pattens also survive today.

Pair of women's silk and leather pattens
British, 1730s

Given by Miss Muriel Gardiner
T.197:C-1927

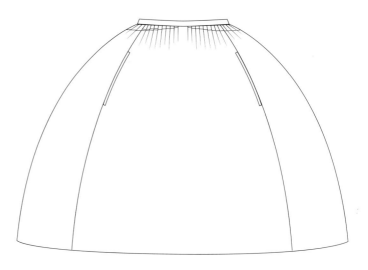

Woman's silk petticoat
British, 1750s

Given by Mrs Baker
T.247–1959

Quilting was a popular means of adding decoration and warmth to garments in the eighteenth century, and many quilted petticoats survive in museum collections. These usually have a layer of wool batting sandwiched between a backing of woven wool or linen, and a top fabric of silk, wool, linen or cotton. Widths of each fabric were sewn to form a long rectangle and the three layers put together, set in a frame and then quilted. The sewing of the petticoat's back seam and shaping of the waist were done after the quilting.[3]

Quilted petticoats could be made bespoke or at home, or even be bought ready-made. Trade cards of eighteenth-century milliners, haberdashers, linen-drapers and mercers advertise a range of ready-made quilted garments, including gowns, bed gowns, waistcoats, petticoats and baby clothes (see page 13).[4] Petticoats were probably sold flat or with only the back seam stitched, allowing the waist to be finished and the length adjusted to fit the wearer.

This example is made of six widths of silk and its design is typical of eighteenth-century quilting, combining floral motifs with abstract patterns of diamonds and overlapping shells. The vertical arrangement of the design is slightly unusual: most petticoats have a horizontally oriented pattern with a border at the hem. The petticoat has had an extra strip of a non-matching blue silk added at the waist. It may have been a ready-made petticoat that was slightly too short, or a bespoke one altered later for a taller wearer.

Woman's silk waistcoat front
British, 1750–70

Given by the family of Hugh Parker Mitchell
T.44-1926

As well as petticoats, women wore quilted bodices, waistcoats, pockets (see page 79) and stomachers. This waistcoat front is quilted in a simple overlapping shell pattern stitched in blue silk thread on white silk satin. A narrow border of embroidery with spangles and chenille thread edges the neck, fronts, hem and belt. The quilting is backed with linen; there are no signs of any wadding.

This waistcoat is unfinished; it has no back, nor does it appear to have been sewn to one. The flat shape of the front in the photo above belies the silhouette the waistcoat would have had when worn. When the top two buttons are fastened, the front curves as if over the upper edge of a pair of stays. When the edges are placed where the sides seams would have been, the wide, flat front conforms to the columnar shape of mid-eighteenth-century stays.

The waistcoat front was a gift to the V&A from the family of Hugh Parker Mitchell. He joined the museum in 1871 and was promoted to Keeper of Metalwork in 1924, but died suddenly in 1926. His wife donated the waistcoat to the Textiles Department in his memory.[5]

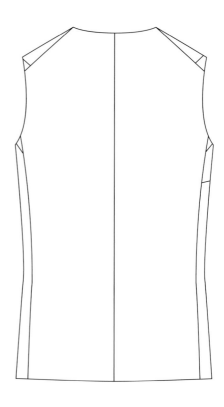

Man's silk waistcoat
British, 1790s

552–1896

An eighteenth-century man's wardrobe included quilted waistcoats and nightgowns (or banyans). In this example, the quilting follows the decorative conventions for waistcoats, with the design arranged along the front edges and hems, and a repeated motif filling in the rest of the front. The quilting is very simple: a border of diamonds along the front edges and at the hem, with parallel lines filling the sides of the waistcoat. This is enhanced with narrow edgings of simple embroidery. Typical of a 1790s waistcoat, it is hip-length, with a straight hem and pockets, and double-breasted with wide revers.

Woman's silk redingote
Italian, 1780s

106-1884

This gown has been remade from another textile, probably a bed cover. The dense, large-scale pattern of interlaced ribbons, flowers and scrolls worked in corded quilting is similar to the designs of woven silks made between 1720 and 1740. The front edges and hem of the skirt preserve the corners of the original coverlet; the sleeves and collar are heavily pieced.

'Redingote', deriving from the French pronunciation of 'riding coat', is the name given to gowns with long sleeves and collars in the style of a man's coat. They were fashionable in the 1780s, when English styles became popular in France – a style known as *anglomanie*, which then spread to Europe and back to Britain. The gown was purchased from a dealer in Milan in 1884.

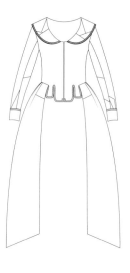 

Woman's linen gown
British, 1775–80

759-1907

Corded quilting uses a cord or thick thread instead of wadding to pad between the layers and define the shape of the stitching. This gown has been recycled, probably from a bed cover of the 1740 or 1750s; one edge of the cover forms the hem of the skirt, with a pattern of densely corded concentric curves with stylized fruits and flowers. Above the border float more corded floral and fruit motifs.

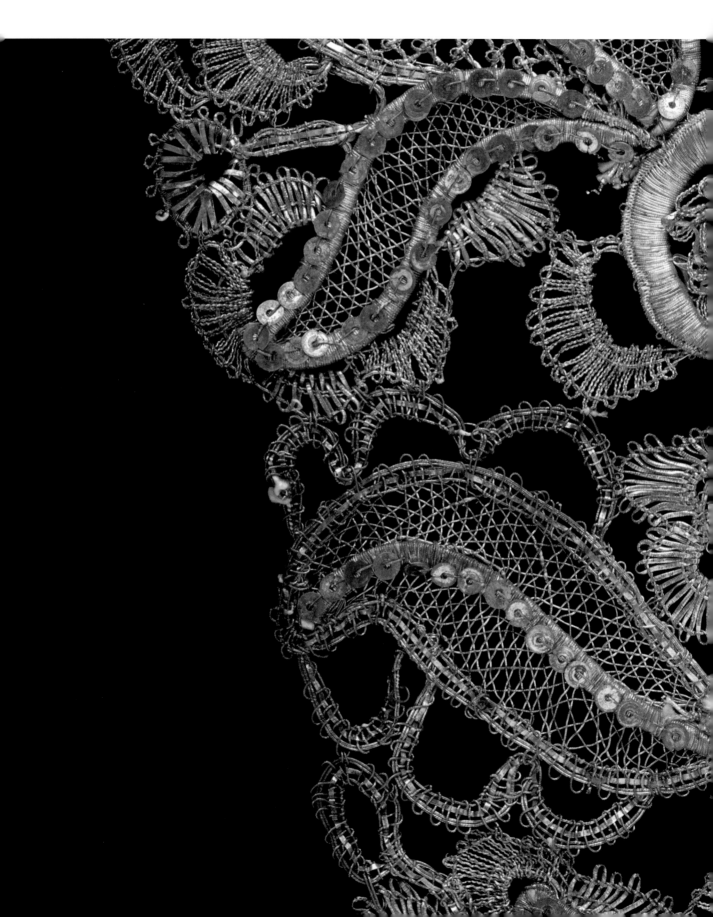

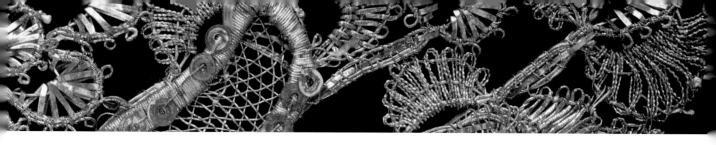

4. Lace and Whitework

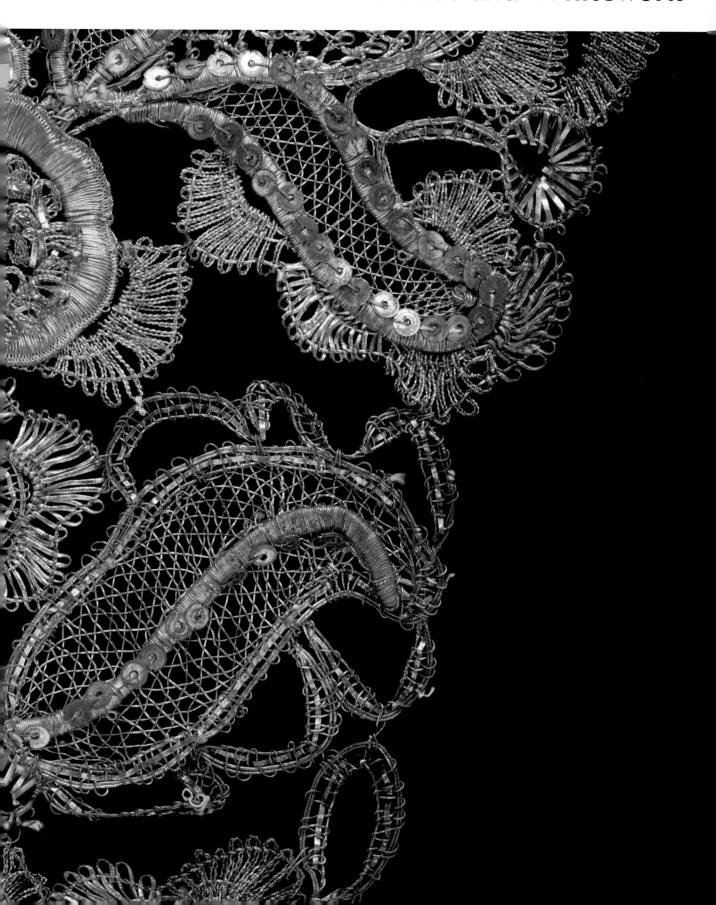

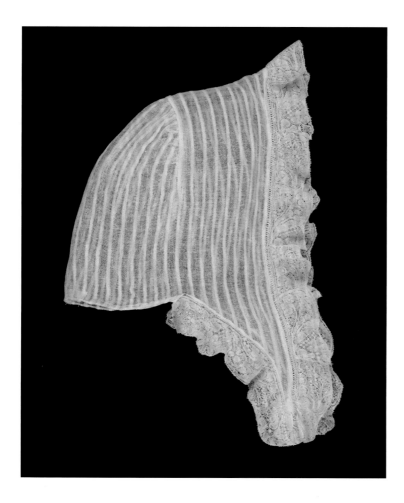

A border of fine Valenciennes bobbin lace edges a cap made of sheer Indian muslin with a narrow self-stripe. It is an unusual survival, as typically once a cap was worn out and/or no longer fashionable, the lace would be unpicked to be used on another accessory and the muslin recycled.

Lace made in Valenciennes in northern France was the most intricate and expensive type in the eighteenth century. Its use of extremely fine threads allowed the creation of a very dense pattern that remained light and delicate. Up to 800 threads could be used to make a piece of lace 10 cm (4 in) wide, each of which would have been worked into the pattern. Consequently, the lace took a long time to make, which accounted for its high price. In 1762 a garniture (cap back, frill, lappets, triple sleeve ruffles and neck edging) of Valenciennes cost between 700 and 1,200 livres.[1]

Covering the head was considered essential in the eighteenth century, for propriety as well as health. While for the most formal occasions a head dressed with ribbons and jewels sufficed, during the day more substantial covering was required, offering opportunities to wear fine linens or imported Indian muslins and the most stylish lace. A cap similar to this one can be seen in the Scottish painter Allan Ramsay's portrait of his first wife, Anne Bayne, painted around 1739.

Woman's cotton cap
British, 1730–50, with French lace, 1730s

T.307-1982

Bobbin lace lappet

French, 1720s

Bequeathed by Mrs Tonge
T.335-1913

The design worked in this Valenciennes lace lappet
is composed of two interlaced ribbons, one narrow
and arranged in sharp zigzags, the other broad
and curving. The latter bears sprays of pineapple
and carnation, as seen in the detail, as well as pear
and pomegranate. Typical of other 1720s lace patterns,
it imitates closely the designs of woven silks.[2]

 Lappets were worked in pairs as a single piece
of lace, with a narrow border in the centre. The border
was sewn to the front of a small cap, with a lappet
falling on either side. Together with a matching lace
back for the cap, they were known as a 'lace head',
a fashionable form of women's headwear in the
eighteenth century.

Bobbin lace lappet

English, 1740s

Given from the Comnène-Everts-Logan Collection
T.9:2-2003

While France and Flanders led in the manufacture
of fashionable lace, English bobbin lace also achieved
a high quality of work, as seen in this lappet. Some
of England's finest bobbin lace was produced in
Honiton in Devon. Made in imitation of Flemish
bobbin lace, this lappet achieves an attractive
combination of crisp outlines and subtle patterns
against a translucent ground.

 Lappets could be worn in a variety of ways, either
hanging down on either side of the cap to frame
the face, or pinned up. This style of headwear could
also be made of whitework or other lightweight,
diaphanous materials.

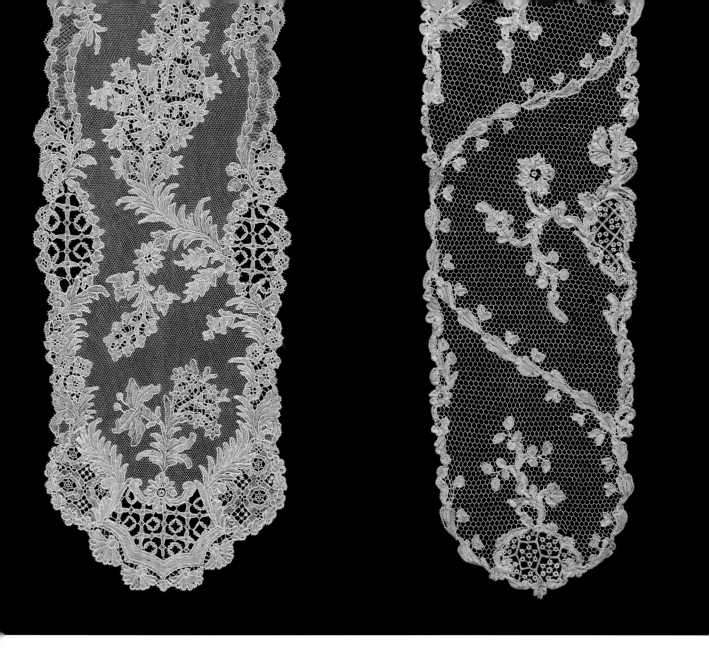

Needle and bobbin lace lappet
Flemish, 1750s

Given by Margaret Jardine
T.107-1916

This lappet is a combination of a bobbin lace ground with motifs worked in needle lace, made separately and then sewn together, probably by three different craftswomen. Brussels had been a leading centre of lace production since the early seventeenth century, making both bobbin and needle laces. Brussels lace was prized for the variety of patterns worked in its motifs and for the exceptional fineness of the linen thread used, which gave it a transparent quality.

By the mid-eighteenth century, the designs were no longer as dense as those of earlier lappets. The influence of the Rococo style on lace led to smaller motifs and more open patterns worked against larger areas of background.

Needle lace lappet
French, 1760s

277:A-1890

The villages of Alençon and Argentan in Normandy were important centres of the French needle lace industry. A characteristic of their production was a fine hexagonal mesh of twisted button-hole stitches. This gave them an openness and delicacy of design that became fashionable as Neoclassical design began to influence lacemaking, reducing the size of motifs and increasing the areas of plain ground. Here the edges of the motifs are worked slightly more thickly than those in the centre, giving the lappet a degree of texture.

Bobbin lace border
French, 1720s

Given by Margaret Simeon
T.138-1992

Lace was an important accessory for men in the eighteenth century. Court and formal dress required that lace ruffles (gathered borders of lace) be worn around the cuffs of a linen shirt and along its front opening (known as a 'bosom ruffle'). The width of these ruffles can be estimated by looking at portraits of men wearing lace and calculating the proportion of it covering their hands. They were probably between 5 cm (2 in) and 8 cm (3 in) wide, making the examples shown here suitable for adorning a man's shirt or trimming a woman's cap or apron.

This border was made in Binche, a small lacemaking village near Valenciennes, producing bobbin lace in a similar style. The very fine threads and dense texture of the pattern are similar to those of the Valenciennes lappet on page 100, left.

Bobbin lace border
Flemish, 1730-50

Given by Margaret Simeon
T.139-1992

Mechelen was a small lace-making town in Flanders, between Brussels and Antwerp. Its lace had a characteristic style that used a distinctive shiny thread to outline the motifs, as can be seen in this border. The rounded, finished end to the border may have been a feature of men's lace ruffles, as these would have been visible when worn on the cuffs or front shirt opening.

In general, there were no distinctions between the styles and designs of lace worn by men and women, but the specific dimensions and shape of the lace differed when intended for women's sleeve ruffles and shift edgings or men's shirt ruffles. However, the pattern of this border is very unusual, representing an elegant formal garden with low walls, a fountain and a rabbit disappearing down its hole, suggesting it was possibly commissioned by a man to commemorate his newly landscaped estate.

Needle lace border
French, 1740-60

Given by Miss S. L. Bird
CIRC.366-1925

Fashionable lace of the mid-eighteenth century echoed developments in the designs of woven silks, featuring more open areas of mesh ground, highlighting the motifs. In this case, the floral pattern has been worked with a combination of dense stitches as well as a variety of open ones.

All the borders shown on this page have an edging of simple open stitches along one side (those of the top and bottom borders are extremely fine), called either a 'header' or a 'footer', depending on how the lace was worn. This was where the lace would be gathered and stitched to the linen shirt or other accessory, ensuring that the removal and reattachment of the border would not damage the lace structure.

Needle and bobbin lace border
French, 1780-99

Given by Miss C. Southwell
T.361-1988

This border has a ground of bobbin-lace net to which needle lace motifs have been applied. The design reflects the influence of the Neoclassical style, with large areas of net and small, stylized floral motifs, and elongated cartouches along the top edge.

Silk bobbin lace sleeve ruffle
French, 1755–65

1043-1855

White laces were traditionally made of fine linen thread, but this example is made of silk, and its pale colour, 'blonde', gave its name to the lace itself. Although the designs of blonde lace were very simple – diamonds, zigzags and triangles arranged geometrically – its light, sheer texture made it very popular, especially during the second half of the eighteenth century.[3] In this example, a silk chenille thread outlines the motifs, adding subtle texture to the lace.

Sleeve ruffles were an important accessory in women's fashion, and many laces were made specifically in scalloped shapes of increasing size, to be worn together in twos or threes. These were sewn to the cuff of a woman's linen shift in order to be visible underneath the sleeve ruffles of a gown, mantua or sack (see pages 56–62).

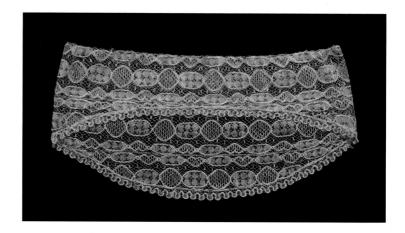

Silver bobbin lace stomacher
English, 1740s

Given by Mrs R. Stock
T.80B-1948

Metal laces were very fashionable in the eighteenth century, particularly for court dress. A stomacher as lavish as this example was probably worn with a court mantua embellished with silver thread embroidery. The same types of thread used in precious metal embroidery (see, for example, page 123) were employed in metal lace. Here, silver filé, frisé, strip and spangles define the pattern of a central rose surrounded by leaves. The thickness of the metal threads allowed only for quite large, simple bobbin lace techniques, but the splendour of their light-reflecting qualities outshines the unsophisticated structure.

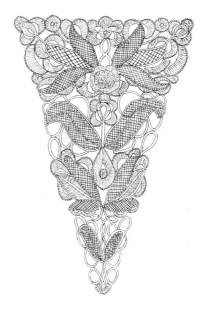

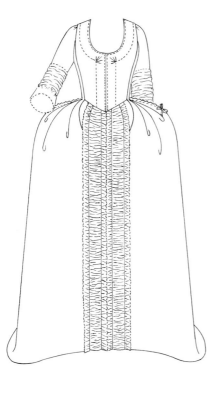

Woman's cotton and silk
robe à la française
French, 1775–80, of Indian muslin, 1770s

T.332-1985

Appliqué and net cleverly imitate true lace on this *robe à la française*, as the British sack was known in France. The motifs are cut out of cotton and sewn with linen thread to a linen net ground. This technique would have been much faster and cheaper than the production of bobbin or needle lace, but achieves the same effect when applied in broad bands to the front edges of the skirt and sleeves of the *robe*. These have been worked to shape; the borders of the front edges narrow from the hem to the waist and from the bodice fronts across the back of the neck.

The *robe* is made of fine Bengal muslin with vertical stripes, a variety of weave known as 'doreas', imported to France through the French East India Company, and the embroidery in cotton thread was tamboured, probably in France.[4] Pink silk lines the robe throughout. It has faded over time even in areas not exposed to light, indicating that the dye was a fugitive one, probably safflower. When new, it would have given a much rosier glow through the muslin and gathered net.

The robe's formal, slightly conservative style, with skirts cut for a wide hoop, has been rendered more up to date by the front closure of the bodice and the use of the fashionable Indian muslin.

Cotton sleeve ruffle

British, 1730s

Given by J. S. Masser, Esq.
T.140&A-1959

Although made using different techniques, whitework and lace shared similar aesthetics and purposes during the eighteenth century. 'Whitework' refers to embroidery using white thread on a white ground, usually cotton or linen. On heavier fabrics, whitework sometimes incorporated corded quilting. On light muslins and lawns, drawn thread and pulled fabric techniques were used to give an open, lacy effect, as seen in this sleeve ruffle, made of Indian muslin embroidered with cotton thread.

At the beginning of the century, whitework was more fashionable than the contemporary heavy styles of lace, so lacemakers strove to imitate its effects. This proved so successful that by the 1730s, whitework was in turn attempting to copy fashionable lace, as seen here in the extensive use of openwork techniques.[5]

Cotton sleeve ruffle

German, 1740s

Given by Mrs Yvonne Coste
T.229-1964

In the eighteenth century, the finest whitework was made in Saxony and sold in Dresden, by which name it was known throughout Europe. This sleeve ruffle exemplifies the quality of Dresden work. A fine 'mesh' background, rivalling that of lace, has been created with drawn thread and pulled fabric stitches in linen thread on cotton muslin. The same technique worked in a variety of patterns fills the centres of the leaves and flowers, whose shapes are outlined to imitate the crisp edges of needle lace (see page 103). Satin stitch and decorative eyelets create the small sprays of berries. The narrow border of bobbin lace was probably added in the nineteenth century.

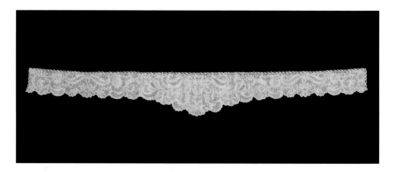

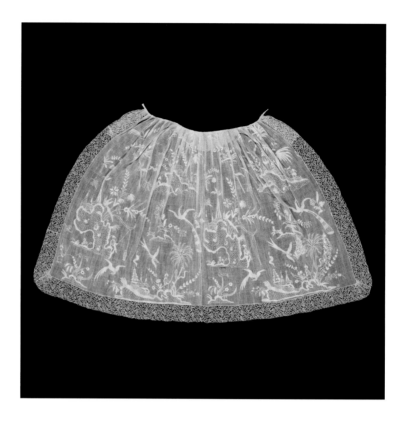

Linen apron
British, 1720–40

Given by Mrs Dora Carson Roberts and
Miss Tufnell
T.9-1952

Elaborate aprons of lace, whitework and silk embroidery (see page 119) were fashionable accessories, worn by women with morning and afternoon dress. These were not the 'protective' sort of apron for housework, but decorative symbols of elite women's skills as domestic managers. This apron is made of linen, either the sheer lawn from Laon in northern France or possibly the fine linen muslin woven in Paisley, Scotland, in imitation of the Indian variety made of cotton.[6]

The apron is edged with a border of Flemish bobbin lace, which was slightly longer than needed. Rather than cut the expensive lace – which could be used again on something else – the extra length was folded under on either side at the waistband. The embroidery, worked in linen thread, includes satin stitch, chain stitch, eyelet holes bound with buttonhole stitch, and French knots, as well as drawn thread and pulled fabric work.

The chinoiserie design of the whitework may derive from a single source or it might have been compiled from several. These sources could include imported Chinese ceramics, lacquer or wallpaper, or European goods imitating Chinese designs. Scenes of fishermen were popular in Chinese decorative arts, as were illustrations of birds. Similarly, a landscape with a craggy promontory revealing the sky behind it through picturesque hollows was a longstanding motif in Chinese art. However, the little rabbits occupying the rocky openings on this apron are a British addition.

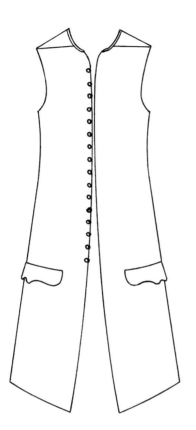
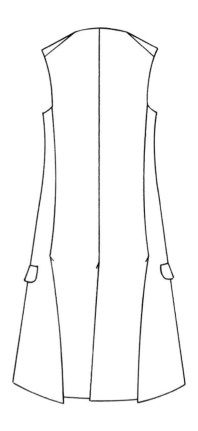

Man's silk waistcoat
British, 1735–40

Given by Mrs Ensor
T.271-1923

The embroidery of this waistcoat is characteristic of Late Baroque design, with a dark-coloured silk densely covered in a pattern of large peonies, roses and tulips. Most of the motifs are couched with silk chenille thread, which has a thick, velvety quality. It was often used in eighteenth-century embroidery; here it adds texture to the ribbed surface of the silk and contrasts with the smooth, floss silk threads in satin stitch used for some of the flowers. Multiple shades of green for the leaves and pinks and blues for the flowers also give depth to the design.

At the beginning of the 1700s, a coat and waistcoat were about the same length, but the latter gradually shortened as the century progressed. The length of the skirts of this waistcoat are typical of the 1730s.

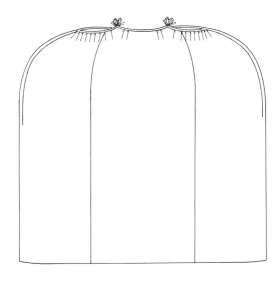

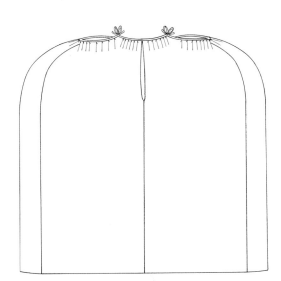

In the eighteenth-century wardrobe, the most lavish decoration was found on court dress. The mantua and petticoat, in particular, offered a broad canvas for embroiderers' skills. The design of this example comprises a border of shaped trellises alternating with urns, worked in silver-gilt thread and thick purl. Large, naturalistic flowers and leaves embroidered in coloured silk threads sprout from the serpentine stems growing out of the urns. The silver-gilt thread has been stitched over shaped pieces of vellum or card to give a slightly raised effect and define the motifs more sharply. The pale silk ground and botanically precise flowers are typical of the British Rococo style. The design is less densely arranged than that on the waistcoat on page 115, but still large in scale.

The embroidery has been carefully designed to accommodate the specific cut of the mantua. It was scaled down to fit the narrow dimensions of the sleeve cuffs and front robings. The corner of the train and the panel below are all one piece. The embroidery is worked on the right and wrong sides of the silk in different areas so that only the right side of the needlework shows when the mantua train is arranged (see page 39).

Extensive alterations were made in the nineteenth century to adapt this mantua for fancy dress, some of which have been reversed to recover as much of its original form as possible, as illustrated in the drawings.

Woman's silk mantua and petticoat
British, 1740s

Given by Miss Katharine Boyle
T.179&A-1959

Man's linen waistcoat
French, 1730s

408–1882

The densely couched, dazzling precious metal embroidery of this waistcoat completely covers its coarsely woven linen ground. A flowing pattern of leaves and flowers has been worked in silver-gilt filé, frisé, strip, purl and spangles. The ground between has been filled with silver filé, over which are small floral motifs embroidered with more silver-gilt thread, purl and spangles. Applying the filé in the technique known in the eighteenth century as *gaufrure* adds a waffled texture to the embroidery.[1] By using very fine coloured silks for the couching threads, white for the silver and yellow for the silver-gilt, the tiny stitches holding the metal threads in place are carefully concealed.

The waistcoat was altered in the nineteenth century, probably for use as fancy dress.

This silk apron, embroidered with silk and silver-gilt threads, would not have been worn for any real housework, but to adorn the day ensemble of the mistress of the house. The design of large-scale flowers and leaves shaded with coloured silks was drawn to fit the wide, shallow dimensions of the apron. Silver-gilt threads were worked in the *gaufrure* technique for the centres of some of the flowers, and couched in spirals for others. The three deeply scalloped sides have smaller scallops and a narrow edging of a vermicelli pattern in silver-gilt thread.

The apron would have originally been gathered and bound with a tape to form the waistband and strings. Although this style of apron eventually went out of fashion, many were preserved for their embroidery.

Woman's silk apron
British, 1740–45

597-1886

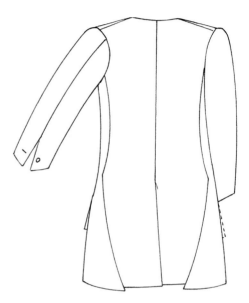

Man's linen waistcoat
British, 1720s

T.125–1938

A pattern of sunflowers, cornucopia and curling leaves, worked in yellow silk, adorns this sleeved linen waistcoat. The ground between is filled with a vermicelli pattern in white silk. The design and materials reflect the complex exchange of influences between Europe and India in the eighteenth century. Embroideries worked on white calico with tussar (wild silk) thread – whose natural colour was a shade of yellow – were a popular style of Indian export, made in Bengal originally for the Portuguese market. The source of inspiration for this British waistcoat could have been either an Indian export textile or a Portuguese garment. The spiky leaves are characteristic of Indian export needlework, although they were originally inspired by English furnishings sent to India in the late seventeenth century for Indian embroiderers to follow. The sunflower was a popular English motif and the rather strange lattice-filled cornucopia may be an echo of the unusual architectural shapes seen in a style of woven design popular between 1709 and 1712.

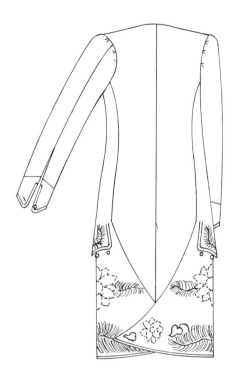

Man's silk waistcoat
French, 1730s

252-1906

Men's court dress was as sumptuously decorated as that worn by women. This sleeved waistcoat of the 1730s is embroidered with coloured silks and silver threads, including filé, frisé, strip and purl. The heavy borders of plain silver thread have been worked over pieces of shaped parchment or card. The waistcoat is unusually lavish: expensive yellow satin has been used for the back of the garment as well as the sleeves. Because a coat was always worn over them, waistcoat backs were normally made of plain linen or wool.

The vivid hue of the silk satin was probably inspired by the yellow of Chinese imperial robes, a very exclusive colour in China. Although worked in much more luxurious materials, the waistcoat bears the same sunflowers as the informal linen waistcoat on page 121. It is also decorated with spiky leaves similar to those on the previous page, revealing the circuitous route of design influence, from seventeenth-century English furnishings to Indian export textiles, which in turn inspired French court embroidery.

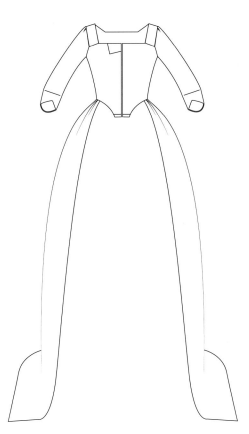
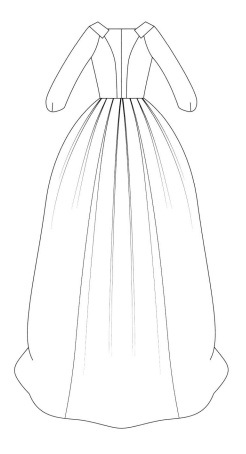

By the end of the seventeenth century, Britain had been granted trading privileges by the Qing Empire of China and the British East India Company began importing porcelain, lacquer, tea and textiles. The latter included many plain satins and taffetas as well as damasks, brocades and embroidered silks.[2] Unlike embroidery for dress produced in Europe (see pages 75, 126, 127 and 202), which was worked only in the areas drawn by the tailor or mantua-maker, whole lengths of silk were embroidered in Guangdong province to be purchased in England and made into any garment.

The craftsmen of Guangdong followed British designs sent by the East India Company to suit British tastes, as in this example, a pattern of whimsically coloured convolvulus, carnation, marigold and various fruit blossoms. The narrow gap, or void, of satin fabric left between the embroidered areas within the motifs is characteristic of Chinese production, as is the width of the silk.[3] At about 71 cm (28 in) from selvedge to selvedge, silks woven in China were much wider than European silks (which were between 48 and 54 cm/19 in and 21 in).[4] The embroidery is very accomplished and has been identified as dating from the Qianlong period (1735–96).[5]

The gown was made in the early 1780s; the front-closing bodice with a point at the centre-back waist was fashionable at the time. Later in the decade, the waist seam at the back was unpicked and the waistline raised. Like the Indian embroideries on pages 128 and 130, this textile may have been made as a furnishing textile, although there are no signs of any other use of this splendid embroidered silk before it was made into a gown.

Woman's silk gown
British gown, 1780s, Chinese embroidered silk, 1760–80

Given by the Green Family
T.55-1973

Panel of silk for a woman's shoe

British, 1720s

Given by Miss C. E. Keddle
231–1908

This scrap of plain silk has been embroidered for use as the upper and heel quarters (worked as one piece) of a shoe. The shoemaker drew out the shapes of these pieces so that the embroiderer could work only the areas needed. A pattern drawer, of the kind described on page 13, probably devised the design of stylized flowers and leaves, which the embroiderer worked with French knots, outline, stem, short, satin and cross stitches in brightly coloured silks.

By the late eighteenth century there was a prototype of 'assembly-line' production for the decoration of men's court suits (coats, waistcoats and breeches) as well as individual waistcoats. As described on page 75, shapes were sold to customers all over Europe and then made up by their tailors. This industry included many pattern drawers, who drew and painted in watercolours the great variety of new and fashionable designs for embroiderers to work.[6]

The 1750s waistcoat on page 75 (below) required two widths of silk, one for each side. By the 1780s, the waistcoat had shortened to hip length, with much narrower skirts, so embroidery for both fronts would fit on one width of silk. This 1780s shape includes two fronts (the right-hand one with seven uncut buttonholes and a separate skirt), two collar and two lapel corners, and small sprigs for the buttons. The two pocket flaps were embroidered separately and are already sewn to the waistcoat fronts.

Man's waistcoat shape
French, 1780s

Given in memory of Miss Amelia Harjes, Paris, 1880–1967
T.427–1994

Woman's cotton petticoat

British, 1780s, of Indian embroidered
calico, 1740s

1324:A-1901

This petticoat and its accompanying gown are an example of the
embroideries in very fine chain stitch worked with a needle for which
the Gujarat region of India was renowned. The large-scale pattern
with intricate flowers and spiky leaves was a style of mid-eighteenth-
century Indian export embroidery, inspired by seventeenth-century
English crewel needlework for furnishing textiles (see page 127).[7] It was
probably used first as a furnishing textile before being converted to a
gown and petticoat in the 1780s. Both garments are heavily pieced.

Indian chain stitch embroideries were very popular in Britain and much copied. This sleeved waistcoat dates to the 1740s and although worked on cotton, the worsted embroidery thread identifies it as British, as this type of wool was never used in India. The pattern, however, is inspired by Indian textiles; the curving, spiky leaves and large bulbous flower of rounded petals shown here echo those on the calico petticoat on the left.

Man's cotton waistcoat
British, 1740s

Given by Miss K. A. Sauvary
T.217-1953

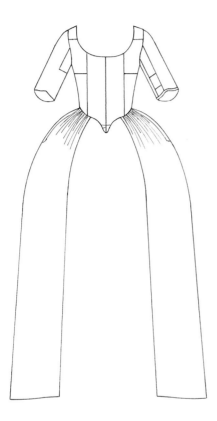
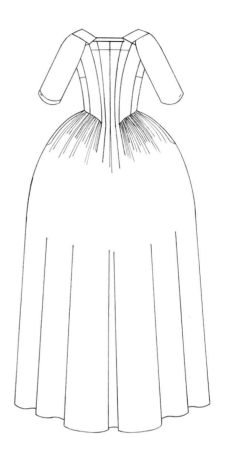

This gown is another example of the exceptionally fine embroideries, chain stitched with a needle, that were produced in Gujarat. The embroidery is another type of imported furnishing fabric, similar in date to the one on the previous page but very different in style. Here, the design is influenced by late seventeenth- and early eighteenth-century British bed curtains and coverlets embroidered with individual floral motifs.

By the 1770s the designs of fashionable English silks featured single floral motifs arranged against a plain ground. This style of Indian embroidery would therefore have been very appropriate for dress, even though it was made as a furnishing textile. The stylized carnations, roses and small birds were also in harmony with the trend towards more abstract motifs in the 1770s. The bodice has some piecing, but the pristine condition of the embroidery suggests it had no prior use as a furnishing.

Woman's cotton gown
British, 1775–80, of Indian embroidered calico, 1740–60

Given by Mr and Mrs G.H.G. Norman
T.391-1970

Woman's silk petticoat
British, 1780s

T.79:A-1963

The technique of chain stitch done with a hook spread to Europe sometime during the 1750s.[8] It was called tambouring, after the drum-shaped frame called a tambour, from the French for 'drum', in which the fabric was held. The speed with which tambouring was executed and the fineness of its stitches made it a popular choice for decoration in the late eighteenth century, as this petticoat demonstrates. The white silk ground and light palette reflect the influence of Neoclassical design. Although decorated with floral motifs, these are highly stylized, without the botanically inspired naturalism of the Rococo period. The embroidery is enhanced with applied silk ribbon and blonde lace.

This petticoat appears to have been part of a court mantua, similar in style to the one on page 186 (below). The ensemble was heavily altered in the 1880s to make a fancy dress outfit. The bodice and train of the mantua were cut into two pieces, so the drawings do not reflect its original eighteenth-century style. Although determining the original construction awaits further research, the decoration remains an accurate reflection of 1780s fashion and a new embroidery technique.

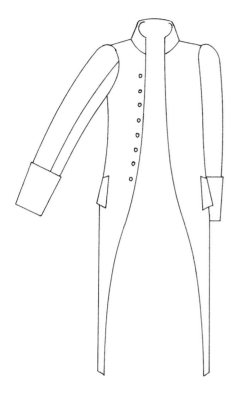
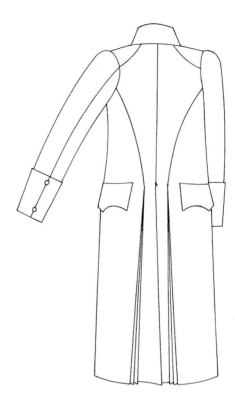

Man's silk coat
French, 1780s

1611-1900

A pattern of floral sprays embroidered with silver-foiled pastes, silver spangles and purl decorates this coat, once part of a court suit. Glass paste was first developed as a substitute for diamonds in the 1670s and became very popular for jewellery in the eighteenth century. Paste usually had a backing of thin metal, either silver to heighten its brilliance, or coloured foil to imitate other precious stones. From the 1770s, pastes were also used in embroidery, in the same manner as spangles and foils. Those on this coat are faceted to imitate diamonds; most are now crazed or clouded, but when new they would have sparkled brightly. The colour of the velvet was once turquoise, but the silk pile threads have uniformly faded to a greenish hue, possibly because the dye was fugitive. When Beatrix Potter visited the V&A in 1903 to look for inspiration for illustrations to a new edition of her children's story *The Tailor of Gloucester*, she was shown this coat.[1] It appears as the backdrop to an image of a little mouse dressed in an eighteenth-century short sack, petticoat and mob cap. Potter has captured its original colour, which still can be seen under the pile in protected areas of the velvet.

Man's silk waistcoat
British, 1780s

Bequeathed by Miss A. C. Innes
T.346–1972

On this waistcoat, the pastes have an iridescent metal backing and smooth surface in imitation of a cabochon opal – a rare and desirable gem in the eighteenth century. The pastes form the centre of some of the flowers, their edges covered with silver purl, now badly tarnished. Elements of Rococo style remain in the design, particularly the ribbon motif and still identifiable species of flowers. The waistcoat was probably once part of a court suit.

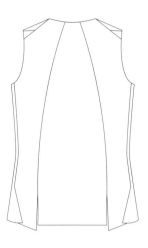

In the decade between the making of this waistcoat and the one on the opposite page, much had changed in both style and decoration. By the 1790s, the skirts of the waistcoat had vanished, replaced by a straight hem at hip level. The pocket had lost its shaped flap, replaced with a rectangular border at the lower edge of the opening, and deep revers turn back on each waistcoat front. Here, silver-gilt spangles are arranged in swags and vertical lines, while tiny sprigs of purl and pastes offer the abstract suggestion of floral motifs. The pastes are faceted and backed with silver to give a diamantine glint.

Man's silk waistcoat
British, 1790s

Given by Mrs R. M. Woods
T.19-1950

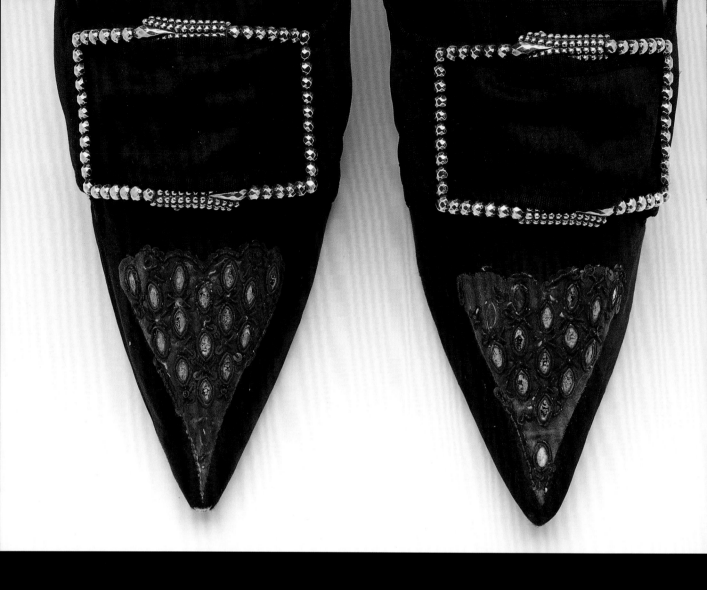
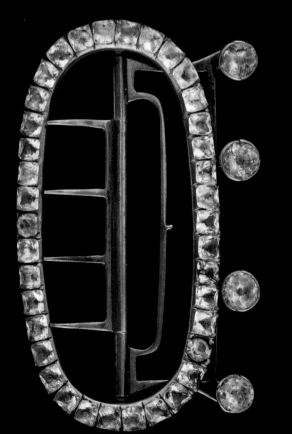

Oval pastes, faceted and backed with silver, decorate the red silk appliqué on the toes of these shoes. The square buckles are made of faceted silver, in imitation of the cut-steel technique, which itself was intended to mimic the sparkle of diamonds.

The advent of fashion labels began in the late eighteenth century when shoemakers started to put their names inside the shoes they made. This pair is labelled 'SUTTON, Shoe Maker To Her Royal Highness the Duchess of Cumberland, Henrietta Street, Covent Garden, London' on the insole, and inside the left shoe the wearer is identified: 'Rebecca Ribblesdale, 1797'.

Pair of women's silk shoes with silver buckles
British, 1797

Buckles given by Mrs John Hull Grundy
266&A-1899 and CIRC.44&A-1965

The stock was a gathered strip of linen that was worn around the neck, over the collar of a man's linen shirt (see page 85), and it was often held in place with a buckle. This example is decorated with faceted, silver-foiled pastes to imitate diamonds. Its length relative to its width and the four studs on one side distinguish it from a shoe buckle. The studs went through the buttonholes at one end of the stock, the prongs going through the linen at the other end to hold it firmly.

In the eighteenth century, shoes were usually fastened with buckles, which held the latchets (straps fastening a shoe over the instep) in place. The pastes on this example are foiled with silver, and the flat facets at the bottom of each were painted with a black spot to make them glitter like diamonds. The buckle would have been one of a pair, probably for court dress, and may have had matching, smaller buckles to fasten the breeches at the knee.

Man's silver and paste stock buckle
British or French, c. 1780

Given by Pamela Clabburn
T.12-1980

Silver and paste shoe buckle
British, 1770s

Given by the Rev. R. Brooke
947:A-1864

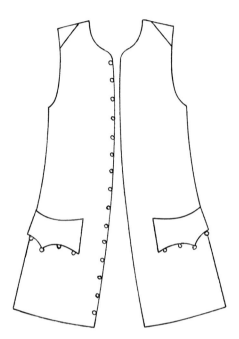
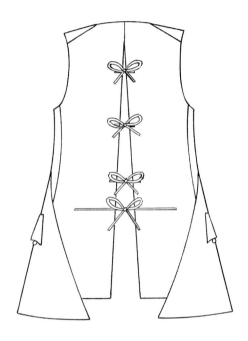

Man's silk waistcoat
French, 1760s

1571:A–1904

Eighteenth-century embroidery was often enhanced with foils. These were made from thin sheets of metal, commonly silver or brass, which were usually gilded or enamelled in a variety of colours. Simple floral or leaf shapes were stamped out and holes punched around their edges so that they could be sewn to fabric. A border of metal purl was worked around the perimeter of the foil to hide its raw edges.

This waistcoat is decorated with large gilt-brass foil flowers. The embroidered decoration of foils, chenille threads, silver strip, silver-gilt purl and spangles is not stitched directly on to it; instead, it was worked on linen, then cut out and applied to the silk, itself a complex weave of horizontal stripes and floral motifs.

The waistcoat has an accompanying coat and likely once had matching breeches. Both the coat and waistcoat have undergone much alteration; they were probably worn as theatre costume in the nineteenth century.

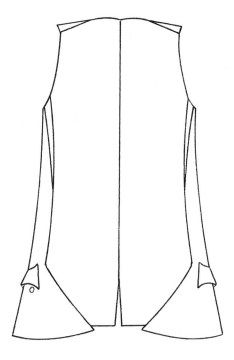

Man's silk waistcoat

British, of French woven and
embroidered silk, 1770s

Given by the Earl of Gosford
T.137–1921

Enamelled red foil, edged with silver purl, and embroidered silver
spangles are the final touches on the intricately woven-to-shape ground
of this waistcoat. A wide, meandering stripe of silver thread is woven
along the front edges and hem, beneath the pockets and on the pocket
flaps. An entwined floral trail in coloured silks and horizontal stripes
of silver strip and silver thread are also part of the weave. By the 1770s,
such an elaborately decorated silk would only have been worn at court.

Man's silk waistcoat
British, 1760s

Given by the children of Paymaster-Capt.
G. W. Osmond RN
T.26:A–1950

The broad streams of silver meandering across this waistcoat are similar to those on the waistcoat on the previous page, but here they are embroidered rather than woven. A net of silver threads has been applied to the silk in a serpentine line, embroidered over with counter-curves of silver purl and spangles. Large silver-foil flowers edged with silver purl mark the intersections of net and embroidery.

An equally lavish coat accompanies the waistcoat. Worn with matching breeches, they would have made a striking suit to wear at court.

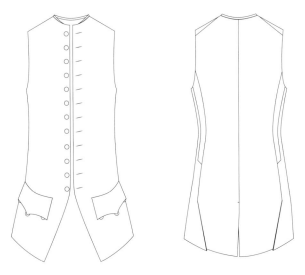

Foils were used in the embroidery of women's clothing, particularly
for court dress, with an effect similar to the waistcoat on the opposite
page. A more unusual application can be seen on this flounce, probably
intended for decorating the front of a petticoat. Swags of flowers
curving between tassels have been painted in bright colours on the silk.
Green and pink foils enhance some of the leaves and petals.

The silk was probably starched or sized first, to prevent the paints
bleeding into the weave. This combination of a thin fabric, a stiffener
and the addition of metal foils is inherently unstable and the resulting
cracks in the silk can be seen in the detail. See also pages 165 and 167
for other English painted silks.

Silk flounce
British, 1780s

Given by Mrs Terry
T.150–1925

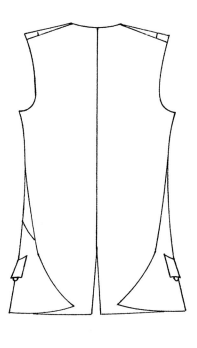

Man's silk waistcoat
British, 1780s, of French embroidered silk, 1780s

Gift of Mrs Phoebe Timpson
T.364-1995

Silver-gilt tissue provides the sumptuous foundation of this court waistcoat. Over it is embroidered a pattern of swags, bows and floral sprays, worked in red and silver-gilt foil, silver-gilt spangles and purl, red and green spangles. Some of the silver-gilt foils are petal- or leaf-shaped; others are curved domes that give the effect of beading. The aesthetic of the design is Neoclassical, but the overall richness harks back to the early eighteenth century, demonstrating the conservatism of court clothing. This waistcoat would have formed the contrasting piece of a court suit, perhaps a red velvet one, as seen in Thomas Gainsborough's portrait of Captain William Wade of 1771, in which Wade wears a similar gold waistcoat.

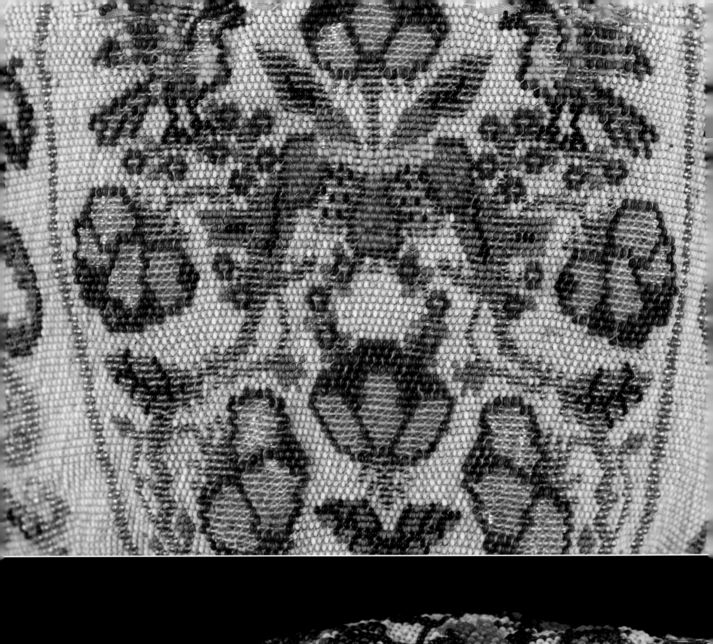

Glass beads were popular decorative elements in eighteenth-century fashion. They were primarily sourced from Venice and Bohemia, although they were also produced in many other countries. The complex systems of bead distribution, as well as the practice of imitating competitors' products, makes it difficult to identify the makers of eighteenth-century beads.[2] On this hemispherical bag, the beads are joined in a woven technique unlike the modern bead-weaving on a loom. They were strung on a thread arranged in a spiral, probably over a mould. Threads from the bottom of the bag run diagonally, crossing over the spiral thread and each other between each bead. The beads vary slightly in size and are made of both opaque and transparent glass.

A design of birds and flowers is worked on two opposite sides of the bag. On the adjacent sides there is a monogram associated with the family Loménie de Brienne, surmounted with a coronet. The bag may have belonged to a relative of Étienne-Charles de Loménie de Brienne, bishop of Toulouse, who was the French minister of finance in 1787–88.[3] The silk band and drawstring are a replacement for the original closure, and the bag has been relined.

Beaded bag
French, 1740s
56-1908

The upper of this shoe is decorated with beads, woven flat in a method similar to the bag above, and sewn around the edges to the leather underneath. Here, too, the beads are of slightly different sizes, in a range of shades of both transparent and opaque glass. The design is a basket from which floral sprays grow, flanked by two birds. A ribbon of silver thread binds the top edge of the upper.

Woman's beaded shoe
French, 1730s
Given by Miss Daphne F. R. Gale
T.102-1971

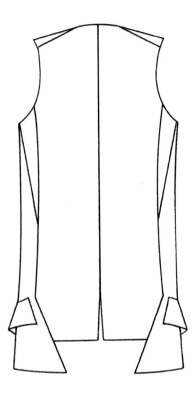
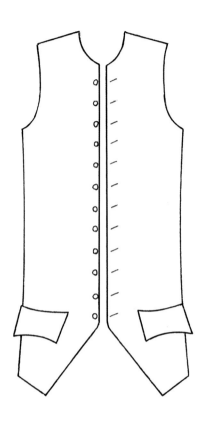

Man's silk waistcoat
British, 1780s, of French embroidered
silk, 1780s

Gift of the Earl of Gosford
T.133–1921

On this magnificent court waistcoat, black and white beads are part
of the embroidery, stitched to the fabric individually in same way as purl
and spangles. Against a pale ground of silver tissue flow parallel lines
of silver-gilt spangles, stitched with black silk in a pattern of alternating
angles and curves. Small sprigs made of silver spangle surrounded by
purl, with black silk stalks, are interspersed between. The pockets and
front edges are bordered with spangles and floral sprigs worked in black
and white glass beads. Along the lower edges, an applied net of silver
thread has been embroidered with waving lines of spangles and the
glass bead motifs. The richness of the materials contrasts with the
restraint of the embroidery pattern and the colour palette, exemplifying
an intriguing blend of up-to-date design on an old-fashioned style.

7. Chintz and Painting

Man's cotton banyan
Probably Dutch, 1750–75, of Indian
chintz, 1750–75

T.215-1992

Painting was a fashionable form of applied decoration, and in the eighteenth century it was influenced by imported fabrics from India and China. Indian chintzes were known to Europe by the late fifteenth century, and the British East India Company began importing them in the mid-seventeenth century from the Coromandel Coast.[1]

Although these cotton fabrics decorated in brilliant colours and intricate designs were described by British consumers as 'painted', they were created by a complicated process of dyeing. First, the outlines of the designs were sketched on the fabric. Areas to be coloured red were painted with an alum mordant and those intended to be black with an iron mordant. The textile was then placed in a chay root dye bath, which coloured both the red and black areas, depending on their mordants. The cloth was washed, bleached, dried and then covered with wax, except for those areas to be coloured blue and green, and placed in an indigo dye bath. The sections to be green were then overpainted with a yellow dye. Starching, beetling and polishing gave the chintz a smooth sheen.[2]

Chintz was so popular that the British government thought it threatened local textile industries, so any form of painted or printed cotton was banned between 1722 and 1774. The dark red ground and large floral motifs are typical of the chintzes made for the Dutch market and imported by the Dutch East India Company, so the banyan was probably made in the Netherlands. A banyan or nightgown was a style of of loose gown that men wore informally at home.

The popularity of Indian chintz inspired European imitations and influenced the styles of European printed cottons. The banyan is lined with a printed cotton, probably Dutch, that bears a floral design adapted from an Indian chintz.

Woman's cotton gown
British, 1795–9, of Indian chintz, 1780s

Given by Margaret Simeon
T.121–1992

After the ban on painted and printed cottons in Britain was lifted in 1774, the legal import of Indian chintzes resumed. Fabrics with a white ground were particularly popular, and this example reflects the response to new developments in British textile design. The scale of the motifs and the serpentine lines reflect the late Rococo designs of 1780s printed cottons. Although hand-drawn, the pattern is remarkably regular. Only close examination reveals the slight irregularities of the repeats – a testament to the extraordinary skill of the Indian artists. A comparison of the colours and pattern of this gown with the banyan on the previous page reveals how carefully the artists accommodated the tastes of different European consumers.

The style of the gown is typical of the late 1790s, with a high waist, long sleeves and a collar. Pleats arranged in groups of three shape the bodice, falling loose at the back into a train. The gown is open at the front, with a narrow belt to close it, and would have been worn with a petticoat. The yellow dye used to create the green shades has faded, leaving only the underlying indigo blue in the stems and leaves.

This gown and two borders in the lace section form part of a splendid collection of historical textiles donated to the V&A in London by Margaret Simeon. A textile designer and teacher at Wimbledon College of Art, she was a discerning collector, acquiring objects that were in pristine condition and that exemplified accomplished artistry and design.

Man's silk nightcap
Italian, 1700–24

528-1898

The technique of painting on silk was well known in Europe and was used throughout the eighteenth century. Painting provided colours and designs similar to embroidery, but could be executed much more quickly and cheaply. A simple pattern of flowers and cherries adorns this nightcap of silk taffeta, which is painted to shape, like the woven waistcoat and embroidered waistcoat shape on page 74. Because the brim and crown are one piece, the former was painted on the wrong side, so it would show when turned up.

Nightcaps were often worn with a nightgown (see page 157). This was particularly important in the late seventeenth century and through the eighteenth, when most men had shaven heads and needed some form of head covering when the wig was not worn, usually at home. The cap was purchased in 1898 from an Italian collector.

The monochrome painting technique used on this silk pocket book deliberately imitates the shading of an engraving or etching. The rustic scene with a windmill and castle evokes the early seventeenth-century Dutch landscape prints that were popular in France in the mid-eighteenth century, in keeping with the taste for pastoral scenes. Bound with a narrow silver-gilt woven lace, the pocket book is lined with pink silk and once had a pink silk ribbon around the silver-thread button. Pocket books were used by men in the eighteenth century to hold papers and/or money (see page 218 for one embroidered with straw).

Silk pocket book
French, 1750s

Given by Miss Florence Kinkelin
T.143–1961

As well as imported Chinese embroideries (see page 125), Chinese painted silks were very fashionable in Europe in the eighteenth century. Guangdong province was the centre of production for most export luxuries, including lacquer and porcelain as well as embroidered and painted silks. As they did for Indian chintzes and embroideries, the East India Company sent patterns and samples of British textiles to be interpreted by Chinese craftsmen.

This gown belonged to Eva Maria Veigel, wife of the renowned actor and theatre manager David Garrick. In November 1755 at the Drury Lane theatre he staged *The Chinese Festival*, an English production of *Les Fêtes chinoises (or Les Métamorphoses chinoises)*, a French comic ballet on a chinoiserie theme.[3] The Garricks were at the centre of London's fashionable creative community and their house in Hampton (a suburb of London) was decorated in the latest styles of furniture and furnishings.[4] Mrs Garrick had a chinoiserie bedroom with Chinese-style furniture made by Thomas Chippendale.[5]

The pale colour of the silk with its painted trails of flowers is typical of Chinese export textiles of the Qianlong period and reflects the Rococo tastes of British customers. In China, the process of painting silks for export began with printing the outlines of the design, which were then covered with white lead paint. The flowers and leaves were delineated with paints made of pigments such as malachite (green), orpiment (yellow), vermilion (red) and indigo (blue), with glue added to thicken them.[6] The final step was painting a silver outline around the motifs. Although the pigments are now much abraded and the silver tarnished to black, when Mrs Garrick wore her dress, it would have been vibrant with colour and gleamed in the light.

Woman's silk sack and petticoat
English ensemble, 1760–65,
Chinese painted silk, 1735–60

Purchased with the assistance
of the Elspeth Evans Bequest
T.593:1&2–1999

Woman's silk gown
Scottish gown of British painted silk,
1780–85

Given by Mrs S. Clutterbuck
T.108–1954

British textile artists were inspired by Chinese painted silks, and there are similarities and differences in style and technique. Chinese painted silks developed from their tradition of calligraphy, while the British method evolved from watercolour painting.[7] In Britain, the silks were prepared with a wash of isinglass (gelatin) and water-based paints applied, in contrast to the white lead and opaque paints used in China (see previous page). This allowed the white of the fabric to create the highlights of the motifs and gave British painted silks a transparent quality.[8]

Chinese artists often copied in an abstract or whimsical way the foreign flowers of the designs they were sent by the East India Company. The flowers on this gown are more botanically correct, with accurate depictions of the pansy, rose, hyacinth, lily and carnation seen here, inspired by popular botanical prints. On the other hand, the butterflies and moths may have been inspired by British entomological publications, but they also resemble in colour and decoration the insects painted on Chinese export china. The skirt and its gathered decoration were painted and trimmed to shape. According to the family history of the donor, this gown belonged to a member of the MacNeil family in Ballymascanlon, Scotland.

Painted silks remained fashionable for several decades. A now obscure novel, *Ermina; or, The Fair Recluse*, published anonymously in 1772, described a fashionable dinner: 'The youngest of these Ladies was dressed in a beautiful painted silk robe; and on her head she wore a large white plume, with several very prettily fancied diamond pins.'[9] In September 1786 the gowns worn by ladies at the royal Drawing Room at St James's Palace in London included 'elegant painted silks'.[10]

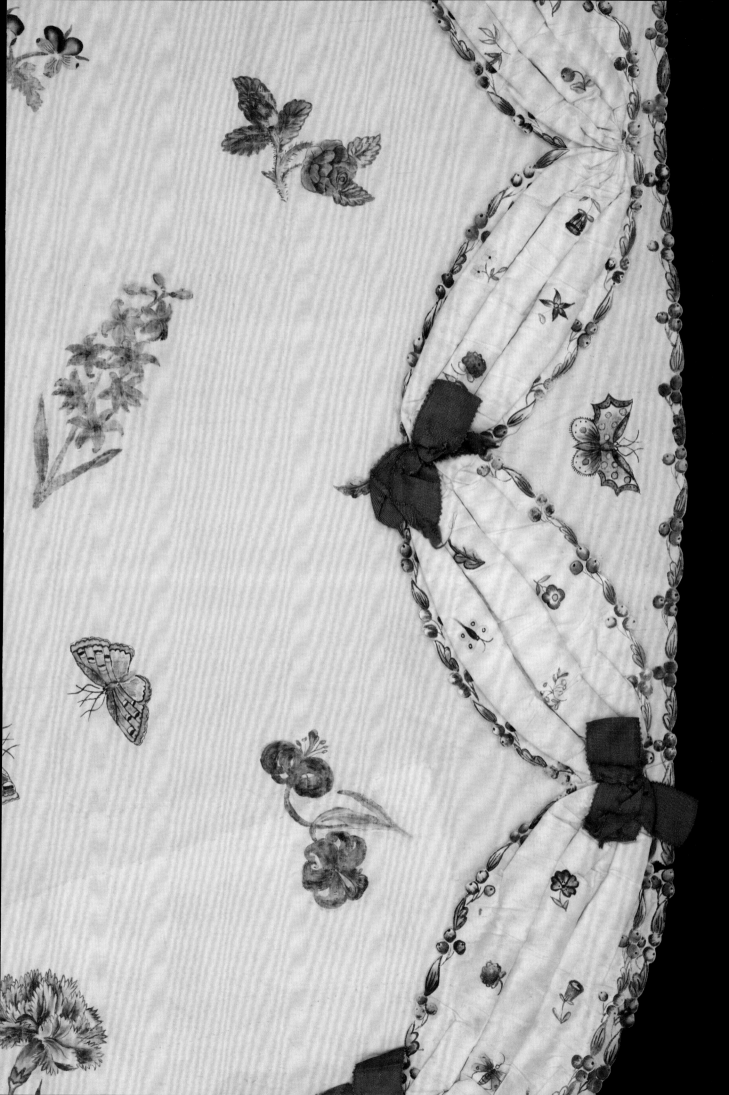

Man's silk waistcoat
British or French, 1780s

256–1880

Neoclassicism is strikingly expressed in the decoration of this waistcoat. The style was inspired by the archaeological discoveries at Pompeii and Herculaneum, and in particular the eight volumes of *Le antichità di Ercolano esposte* (Antiquities of Herculaneum Exposed), published between 1757 and 1792. The waistcoat has been appliquéd with medallions of ivory twill silk, painted with classical images derived from the first three volumes of the book. The two larger medallions below the pockets depict a scene discovered at the Villa Arianna in Stabiae, which also inspired the artist Joseph-Marie Vien to paint his very popular *Cupid Seller* in 1763. Other images, of centaurs, satyrs and Bacchantes (maenads) dancing and making music, are drawn from wall paintings found at the Villa of Cicero in Pompeii.[11] The black ground of the medallions against the figures in white creates the effect of cameos and they appear suspended from floral garlands and bows. These were embroidered in pale greens and blue silks and chenille after the medallions were sewn to the satin ground with a woven stripe.

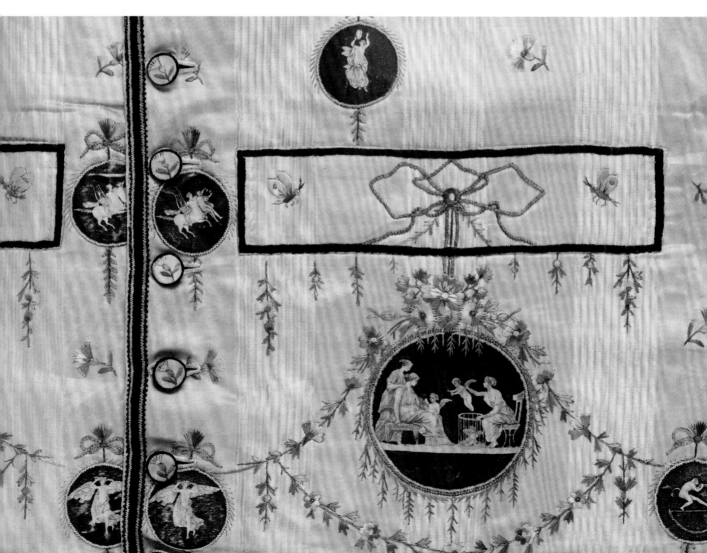

Botanical precision informs this waistcoat, painted with trails of fumitory, clover, borage, pansy, rose, and what may be bird's-foot trefoil around the edges and pockets. It may be professional work; the 'painted Silk Manufacturers' F. & G. Eckhardt & Co. were established in Chelsea and Piccadilly in London by 1791.[12] Such artistry was also executed by amateur painters, including women. In 1762 a 'Gentleman and his Wife' advertised in a Manchester newspaper as tutors, teaching 'drawing and painting Flowers in transparent Colours, upon Paper, Linnen, Silk or Satin, either in the India or English Way, after a Method so particularly easy, that a Lady of tolerable Genius, in three or four Weeks, may learn to equal, or even excel the painted Silks brought from China'.[13] In 1790 a stationer and bookseller in Dorchester, Dorset, included 'Reeves's Superfine Cake Colours for Painting on Silk' in the list of products in his shop.[14] The silk is now very brittle and the waistcoat cannot be turned over to make a diagram or digital image.

Man's silk waistcoat
British, 1790s

T.242-1927

8. Pinking and Punching

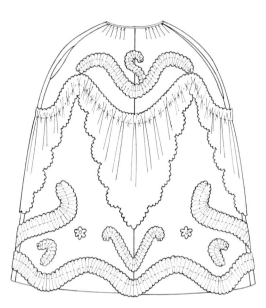

Woman's silk petticoat
British, 1770s

Given by Lt Col. Robert E. Keg
T.60:A-1934

An elaborate pattern of pinking decorates the flounce of this petticoat, as well as the robings and sleeve ruffles of its accompanying sack. Pinking developed as a decorative technique in the early sixteenth century, remaining popular through the seventeenth and eighteenth centuries, and well into the nineteenth. It was usually used on silk and it exploited the fraying of a raw edge. Pinking was created with two different types of tools. One, like an awl, made single holes (two different sizes were used on this garment), and these were sometimes fashioned to create heart- or star-shaped perforations. The other pinking tool took the form of a punch with a straight or curved serrated edge; one of the latter trimmed the edges of the petticoat flounce.

The deliberate perforation of a delicate silk was fraught with hazards. In 1766 *The Female Spectator* bemoaned the damage done to a new suit of clothes during a stroll down the Mall in London when 'a creature, who I afterward heard was a (military) hero, came hurrying along, with a sword as long as himself, hanging dangling at his knee, and pushing roughly by me, his ugly weapon hitched in the pinked trimming of my petticoat, and tore it in the most rueful manner imaginable'.[1]

The fashionable pastimes of the eighteenth century included masquerade parties. With the opening of the London pleasure gardens at Ranelagh and Vauxhall, these were semi-public events. One of the attractions was the opportunity to conceal one's identity and meet people outside one's immediate social circle. This disguise was achieved by either wearing a fancy-dress costume or by donning a mask and domino over one's fashionable clothing. This rare example demonstrates the simplicity of the domino. It is a T-shaped garment with full sleeves gathered at the wrist, large, scalloped, hanging sleeves, a cape and a hood, the edges of each decorated with rows of pinked, gathered ruffles.[2] It is made entirely of pink silk lustring, without a lining or any stiffening, and the layers of the domino would have floated elegantly when the wearer moved. In the 1770s the hood was altered to accommodate the higher hairstyles of the decade.

Dominos were also worn by men. In the portrait by Benjamin West, of Francis Osborne, 5th Duke of Leeds, painted around 1769, Osborne wears a white silk domino over his formal suit. It is similar in style to this one, with the addition of a silver-gilt lace edging. As the selection of garments in this book demonstrates, the colour pink was worn equally by men and women. The portrait also illustrates the increasing height of men's wigs at the end of the 1760s, so this domino could also have been altered for, and worn by, a man.

Silk domino
British, 1765–70

T.195–1968

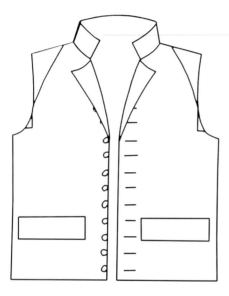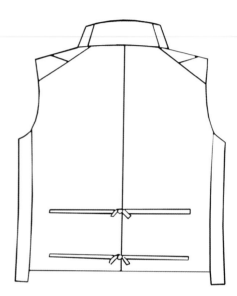

Man's silk waistcoat
British, 1785-90

835-1907

'Punching' was a variation of pinking done when the fraying of the fabric was not desired, as seen on this waistcoat. Examination under a magnifying glass indicates that the perforations were made by fine but rounded teeth, which pushed aside the threads of the silk, rather than severing them. The silk may also have been starched or sized before the pattern was punctured, to encourage the threads to stick together, so that the holes would retain their shape. The continuous repeat suggests that the punch was in the form of a wheel, which created a seamless design along the length of fabric. The silk of this waistcoat may have been woven especially to be pierced. Stripes of satin weave in large squares and small chevrons alternate with ribbed silk dense enough to bear punching without unravelling. The waistcoat fronts are backed with pale blue silk, which shows through the holes, and the overall effect imitates the texture of lace.

Woman's silk kerchief

British, 1770–90

Given by W. A. MacKnight, Esq.
T.314–1920

Punching was also used on women's accessories to create a lace-like texture far less expensively than bobbin or needle lace. Against a dark-coloured gown the finely punched border of this silk kerchief would have imitated a bobbin-made mesh quite convincingly, and its centre is painted with white floral sprigs, mimicking the effect of whitework embroidery. In the eighteenth century, women wore fine linen or silk kerchiefs edged with lace around the neck, tucked into the neckline of a gown, sack, bodice or jacket. The silk of the kerchief was probably sized or starched in preparation for both techniques and is now incredibly brittle.

The term 'punching' for this type of ornamentation comes from an early nineteenth-century description of a shroud 'punched at the edge in a pattern'.[3] Archaeological excavations reveal that eighteenth-century burial textiles such as winding sheets, shrouds and face cloths, of wool or plain cotton, were also decorated with pinked edges and punched designs.[4]

The practice of punching textiles may have developed from pinking, but it may also have been inspired by other paper arts, such as filigree, découpage and mosaic, or by imported Chinese fans.[5] The Chinese art of cut-paper decorations, known as *jianzhi*, was an ancient craft, done by folding paper and either cutting with scissors or punching shaped holes with blades fixed to bamboo tools.[6] Chinese fans with cut vellum and paper fan leaves were imported to Europe as early as the sixteenth century, and European fan-makers adopted the technique, as this example demonstrates.[7] Punched paper was an inexpensive way of imitating lace, and here it echoes the decorative effect of the carved ivory sticks.

Fan of ivory and punched paper
British, 1750–70

Given by HM Queen Mary
T.213–1959

9. Fringes, Ribbons, Tassels and Buttons

Woman's silk sack

British, 1760s

700-1864

The fringe adorning the sleeve ruffles and robings of this sack is made of strands of blue floss silk and white silk partially wrapped with silver strip, loosely knotted together. Short tufts of coloured floss silk, and rosettes made of parchment strips covered with silk and twisted into the configuration of petals, are included in the knots. The sack was probably first made in the 1740s; the embroidery of large flowers and leaves worked in coloured silks and couched silver-gilt strip and filé dates from this decade. In the 1760s it was altered and updated, perhaps for another wearer, and the fringe probably added at this time.

Although this type of trimming is often referred to as 'fly fringe', this term does not appear in print until 1860.[1] Samples of decorative trimmings (see page 10) similar to those illustrated here, bought in the 1760s and preserved in an album of swatches, were described by their purchaser as either 'fringe' or 'trimming'.[2] This type of fringe – and possibly its name – may have been inspired by the artificial flies made of feathers, fur and silk and used as bait by anglers, although so far no eighteenth-century references have been found connecting the two.

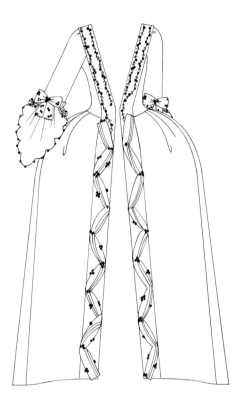

The rosettes in the trimming of this sack are made of concentric circles of tiny loops of floss silk in contrasting or graduated colours of white, pink and maroon. Some are wired in pairs to the fringe, allowing them to stand upright. The fringe itself is made of a core thread of linen wrapped in dark green floss silk and knotted with short tufts of white and green silk. The overall effect, like most knotted fringes, is of a twisting vine sprouting leaves and flowers. The green and white striped silk of the sack is adorned with a variety of flowers embroidered in chenille thread, a floral theme the fringe was chosen to enhance.

Woman's silk sack
British, c. 1770

Given by Miss E. M. Cooke
T.471-1980

Woman's silk mantua

British, 1775–85, of French embroidered
silk, 1775–80

Given by Major W. S. Gosling
T.13–1952

The tangled garden of fringe decorating this mantua is composed of four
strands of wired chenille threads, with wired chenille flowers and leaves
springing from their intersections. Underneath this trimming has been
sewn a narrow border of blonde and chenille bobbin lace. Coloured silk
twist and chenille threads, tamboured in a meandering pattern of flowers,
embellish the white satin of the mantua. The close match of materials
and colours between the fringe and embroidery suggests a collaboration
between weaver and embroiderer, at least in the choice of threads.

Although the quality and style of the embroidery are characteristically
French, the mantua itself is British; this style of garment went out of
fashion in France after the 1720s. The sleeve ruffles show that the silk
was not embroidered to shape. A whole length of silk was tamboured
in France and exported; it was then cut and sewn into a mantua in Britain.
It was probably made in the late 1770s and then modified slightly in
the bodice in the early 1780s. Its petticoat of matching fabric suffered
extensive alterations for fancy dress in the late nineteenth century,
and only a fragment remains.

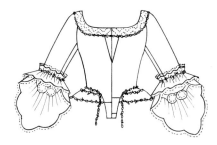

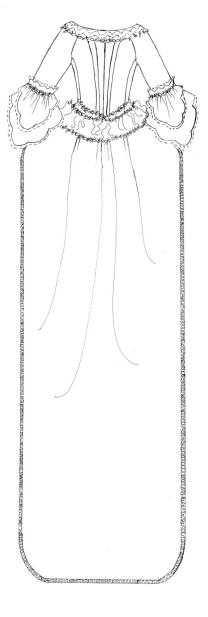

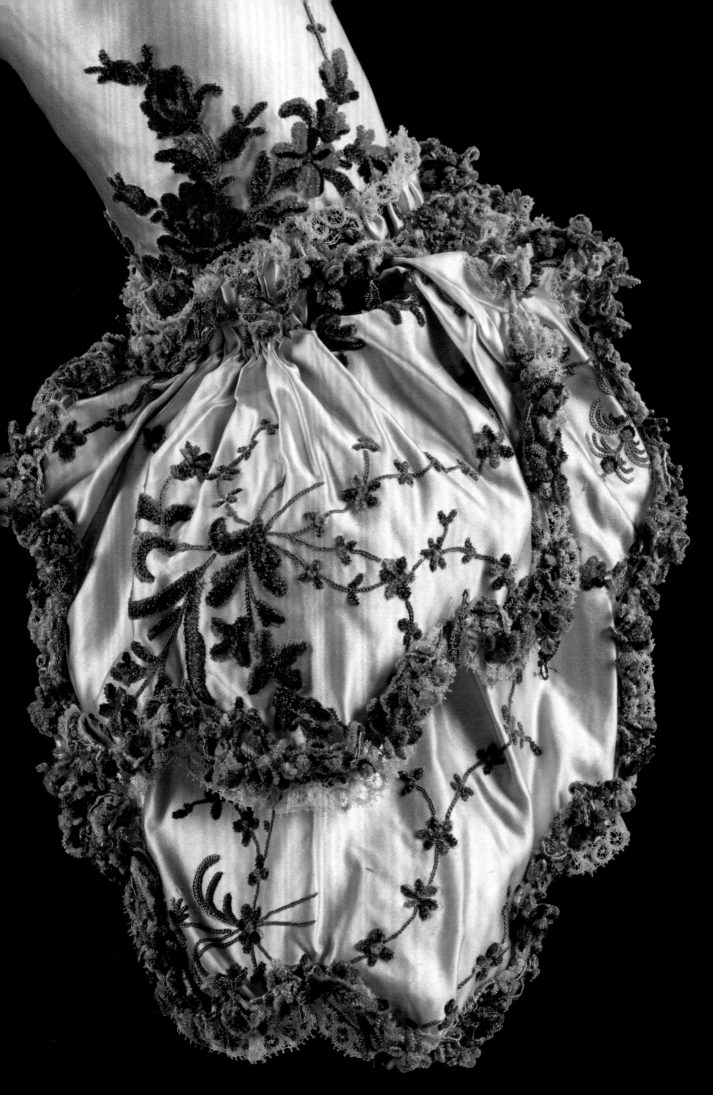

Man's wool waistcoat

British, of a Kashmiri shawl, 1780s

Given by J. Gordon Macintyre
T.440–1966

This waistcoat demonstrates the use of a fashionable imported Kashmiri shawl in men's dress. Two of the decorative corners of a 'moon' shawl form the revers of the waistcoat. The waistcoat fronts have been cut from the patterned ground of the shawl, with its fringe inserted around the revers. Other edges from the shawl's border have been applied to the waistcoat fronts and hems. Unlike the long rectangular Kashmiri shawls that accessorized late eighteenth-century women's fashions, moon shawls were square in shape with a central circular motif.

It seems a rather destructive use of a beautiful imported object to leave out one of its distinctive decorations. Perhaps the shawl was damaged in some way and the unmarred areas salvaged to make an unusual waistcoat.

 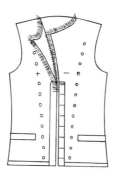

Woman's silk petticoat

British, 1779

Given by Mrs R. Stock
T.80:A–1948

An elaborate fringe of silver threads and strip, interspersed with tassels and headed with a row of silver spangles, embellishes this petticoat. It has a matching gown with a narrower silver fringe on the sleeves and front edges of the skirts. Both are made of a white Spitalfields silk, woven with silver strip in a design of small silver leaves. The ensemble is associated with the marriage of Sarah Boddicott and Samuel Tyssen at St John's church in Hackney on 28 September 1779.[3]

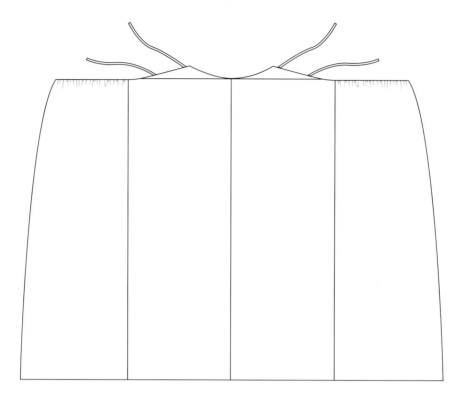

Woman's silk petticoat
French, 1775–80

Given by Miss Louise Band in memory
of Dorothea Crompton
T.180:A-1965

Three-dimensional flowers of pleated grosgrain ribbon, shading from light to dark, accentuate the decoration of this petticoat and its matching gown. More ribbons of blue satin have been applied flat in some areas and padded over wadding in others. The white silk satin of the ensemble is embroidered with silk floss and chenille threads and decorated with a cornucopia of other materials. These include dyed blue feathers, blonde bobbin lace, tassels (probably of dyed straw), and a fringe of dark green silk chenille thread adorned with fake pearls. These last are glass beads lined with 'fish silver' (a slurry of fish scales) to give a pearly effect; four can be seen in the green threads at the right of the image.[4] Only the front of the petticoat has survived, so only the front is shown in the diagram.

Woman's silk petticoat
British, of Chinese silk, 1780s

Bequeathed by Miss Agnes Mary Ralph Kenny
T.98:A-1966

On this petticoat, a broad mauve satin ribbon has been applied flat to edge a wide border of white cotton embroidered with poppies, roses and buttercups. Both are sewn to the hem of the petticoat, which is made of ivory Chinese silk. The same decoration, arranged vertically, edges the front of the matching gown. The rectilinear arrangement of the ribbons and diminutive scale of the embroidered motifs reflect the geometrical influence of Neoclassical design. The petticoat was altered in the nineteenth century to wear as fancy dress.

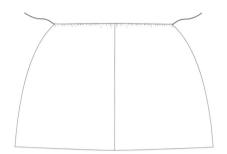 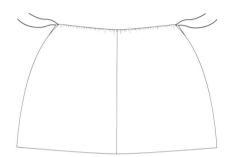

Man's silk waistcoat
British, 1790s

562-1896

Narrow silk ribbon could also be used for embroidery; instead of silk thread, a length of ribbon was threaded through the needle and stitched through the fabric. Here, a design of abstract flowers is worked in chain, outline and satin stitch with blue, white and two shades of brown silk ribbons, with silver spangles.

 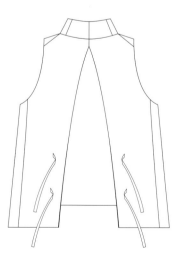

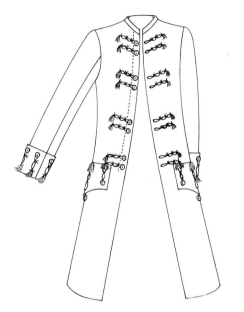 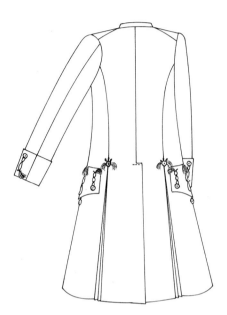

This formal broadcloth day coat is unadorned, except for its buttons and tassels of silver thread, and silver and coloured foil spangles. The tassels hang from the frogging down the fronts, along the pocket flaps and around the cuffs, adding gleam and movement to the plain broadcloth. The frogging is made of silver spangles stitched to narrow strips of thick paper, arranged in simple open twists with the tassels attached at one end. Added lustre is provided by the mother-of-pearl buttons, which are ornamented with tiny coloured pastes around the rims.

Man's wool coat
British, 1770s

Given by Mrs Phoebe Timpson
T.365:1-1995

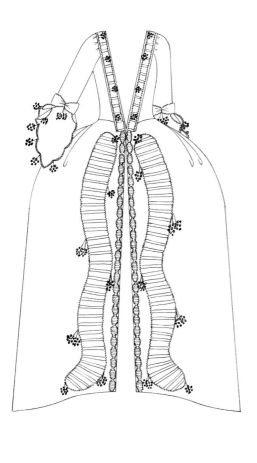

The tassels on the front of this sack are simply dangling lengths of a fringe made of twisted and knotted white and green floss silk, with tufts of yellow and green. Added to these are circles of blue and graduated shades of pink silk, giving the effect of small posies. A second fringe, of white floss silk woven with a twisted silk cord and tufts of green and pink silk, edges the sleeve ruffles and the applied decorations on the sack and its matching petticoat.

The degree to which the fringes match the colours of the sack – made of a Spitalfields silk brocaded with flowers – suggests some sort of collaboration between the weavers of the fabric and the decoration.

Woman's silk sack
British, 1765–70

Given by Miss Galfin
T.12-1940

Tassels were a popular motif in embroidery of the eighteenth century. This formal broadcloth coat is decorated with silver-gilt thread and silver-gilt spangles embroidered over narrow ribbons of very pale pink silk, arranged in a pattern of entwined garlands and festoons. Some of the garlands are caught up by cords ending in tassels, embroidered with silver and silver-gilt purl. Along the bottom of each tassel, a narrow line of red outline stitch is just visible. The buttons are made with silver and silver-gilt foil wrapped over a wooden core, embroidered with spangles, silver, and silver-gilt thread. Although the tassel motif was characteristically Rococo in style, it has been combined here with Neoclassical elements such as the garlands.

Man's wool coat
British, 1770s

656-1898

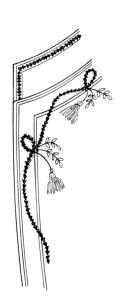

Man's silk waistcoat
English, 1740s

T.94-1931

Buttons were often covered and decorated with
precious metals. Silver foil has been pressed into the
five indentations in the wooden core of the buttons
on this waistcoat. Silver thread and purl have been
applied around the indentations. Such elaborate
buttons complement the dense needlework of the
waistcoat – an early Rococo design of large flowers
and leaves.

    According to acquisition records, this waistcoat
was thought to have been worn by William Morshead
of Carthuther, Cornwall, at his wedding to Olympia
Treise in 1745.[5]

Man's cotton and linen coat
British, 1750s

Given by James Potter, Esq., Master Tailor of Derby
T.962-1919

Plain pewter buttons with a simple, machine-
engraved design finish off this modest fustian coat.
The engraving process was known as engine turning;
the motif was incised by means of a pattern disc,
called a rosette, attached to a lathe. Here, repeating
the engraving in concentric circles has given depth
and texture to the trefoil motif. Engine turning
was used for ivory and boxwood in the seventeenth
century, and by the eighteenth century it had become
a popular method of decorating metals, including
buttons as well as gold and silver boxes. The buttons
are attached in the same manner as the cast gilt ones
on the opposite page, left.

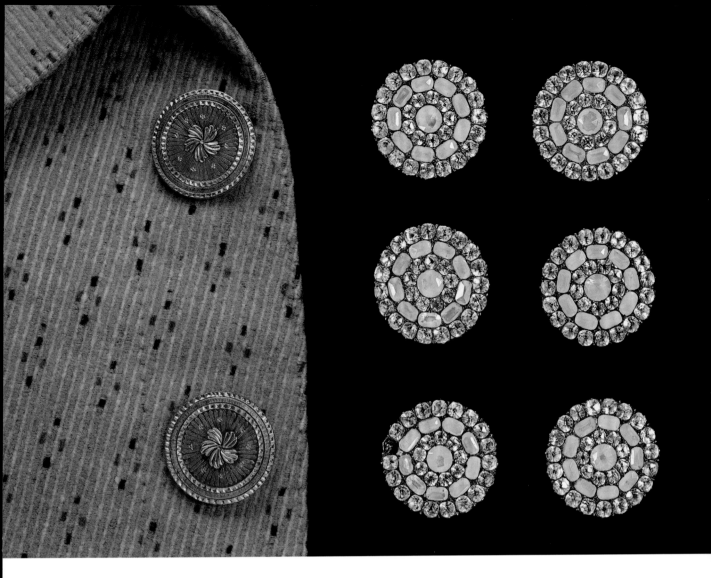

Man's wool coat
British, 1780s

T.358-1980

Twelve gilt-brass buttons embellish this man's
wool coat woven with flecks of blue and red.
Their pattern of a central rosette with radiating lines
wand concentric circles was not made by hand but
created during the casting process. Instead of being
sewn to the coat, the metal shank of each button has
been inserted through a hole in the fabric. On the
wrong side, a narrow strip of leather runs through
an opening in the shank of each button and is tacked
at each end to the interlining, holding the buttons
in place.

Silver buttons set with glass paste
European, c. 1770

Given by Dame Joan Evans
M.154:F, G&H-1975

Men's court and formal coats and waistcoats were
often embellished with jewelled buttons. These were
detached for reuse or recycling of their precious
materials as soon as the garment was no longer worn,
so the finest eighteenth-century buttons usually
survive as separate objects. These six striking opaline
buttons are part of a set of twelve. Opals were rare
before new sources were discovered in Australia
in the 1880s, so many pastes attempted to recreate
their beauty. Here, a milky blue glass has been set
over pink foil to imitate opals, alternating with clear
pastes impersonating diamonds.

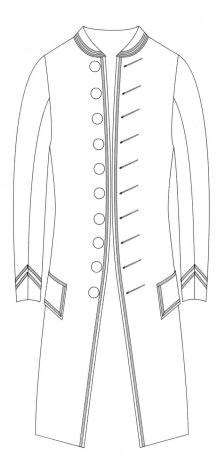
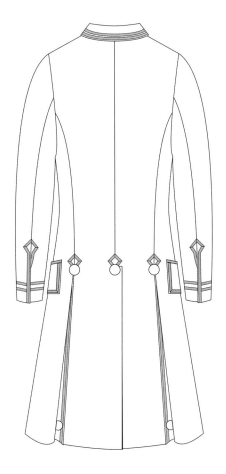

Elaborate buttons are the focus of this otherwise subdued suit. They are made of cast gilt in imitation of filigree over green enamelled foil, in two sizes for the coat and waistcoat. As well as fastening the fronts and decorating the pockets and cuffs, buttons accentuate the top of the side pleats as well as holding them together at the coat hem. A narrow, woven lace of silver thread and strip decorates the front edges and pocket flaps of both garments. The detail also shows the tailor's fine topstitching.

A pair of matching woollen breeches accompanies the coat and waistcoat. The hem and sleeves of the coat have been carefully and discreetly lengthened; the braid was clearly added after this alteration. The silver-gilt lace and enamelled buttons may have been added to enhance an inherited or second-hand suit.

The owner of the ensemble was Joseph Green, Esq., seen wearing it in a now lost portrait on the right. He was a wine merchant in Birmingham and the great-great-grandfather of the donor, Lady Spickernell. Known to have been a dandy, he was nicknamed Beau Green.[6]

Man's wool coat and waistcoat
English, 1760s

Given by Lady Spickernell
T.149&A-1937

Man's silk waistcoat shape
British, 1770s

Given by Dr Margery Simmons
T.26-1961

Buttons were frequently decorated with embroidery.
Waistcoat shapes often included a cluster of small
sprigs, as seen embroidered on the silk satin ground
of this example, to be cut out and used to cover
the buttons. The coat on the right of the opposite
page was probably embroidered and sold as a 'shape',
with its buttons worked in this manner.

Man's silk coat
British, 1775–80

Given by Mrs Phoebe Timpson
T.363-1995

On this coat, the base of the button is formed of
interwoven pink silk thread, silver-gilt filé and silver
strip, onto which are sewn silver spangles threaded
on silver-gilt filé. A narrow, woven lace of white
and yellow silk, silver strip and thread edges the
coat fronts, collar and pockets. Here it reinforces
the top of the pleats and provides a decorative
frame for the button.

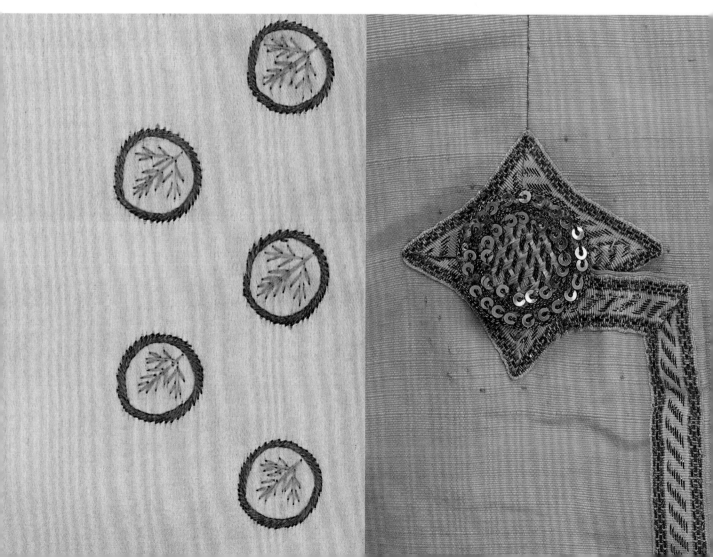

Man's silk coat
British, 1785–90
Given by Mrs N. J. Batten
T.92–1962

The striking combination of colours in the woven silk of this coat is highlighted by the buttons. These have been worked over a flat disc of bone, horn or wood. The design is quartered; each quartering is created by a form of needle-weaving where silk threads are laid side by side and passed over and under each other. The resulting cross shape was also known as a 'death's head'.

Man's silk coat
French, 1790s
106–1891

Buttons embroidered with floss silk, pastes and silver spangles form an integral part of the fine needlework on this court coat. Each has 'spokes' of satin stitch surrounding a mother-of-pearl centre, encircled by now tarnished spangles. The striped silk of the coat has been appliquéd with wavy bands of pink silk overlaid with net, made on a warp frame. Over this ground spreads a pattern of leafy sprays also worked in silk, mother-of-pearl and spangles. Embroidery samples at the Musée des Tissus in Lyon show several remarkably similar patterns, all using applied net with pastes and spangles stitched in comparable designs, also on dark, striped silks.

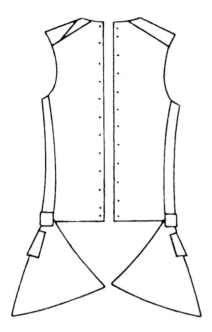

Very few women's garments required buttons in the eighteenth century. Gowns, sacks and mantuas did not fasten with them, although buttons were used for draping the early form of the mantua and later the skirts of a polonaise. From the 1760s, however, buttons began to appear on stomachers, sometimes for fastening (see page 32) and at other times just for decoration. They were also essential for those garments fashioned after men's clothing, such as riding jackets and waistcoats. The very fine silk fabric and silver-gilt embroidery of this waistcoat contrast with the more practical wools and linens of which riding habits were usually made. The core of each button, shaped like a custard squash, is wound with silver-gilt strips and threads. The chain stitching on the waistcoat was worked with a needle.

The drawings show that the waistcoat is in two pieces, lacing up at the back, which suggests that even here, the functional buttons and buttonholes were more for decoration and that the garment was routinely fastened at the back.

Woman's silk waistcoat
British, 1760s

Given by T. J. Edward
T.155-1979

Woman's silk mantua
English, of French silk, 1760s

T.252-1959

The use of fur in eighteenth-century fashion is difficult to illustrate as it appears infrequently in portraiture and most of the garments made of fur have long since succumbed to moth. This mantua combines both a fur motif and real fur in an unconventional – to modern tastes – manner. The silk is brocaded in a pattern of an undulating band of ermine (see top right) with floral motifs, worked in coloured silks and silver-gilt thread. The rich colours of the ground and motifs identify the silk as French. The fur motif was a popular one, and a Lyons silk merchant's sample book dated 1763–4 includes a swatch of brocaded silk with a similar pattern of ermine tails.[1] Even more striking is the addition of real ermine tails to the silver bobbin lace decorating the front robings. Ermine fur had a long association with royalty due to its rarity: only in winter did the wild stoat's coat provide the contrasting white fur with black-tipped tail that gave ermine its distinctive appearance.

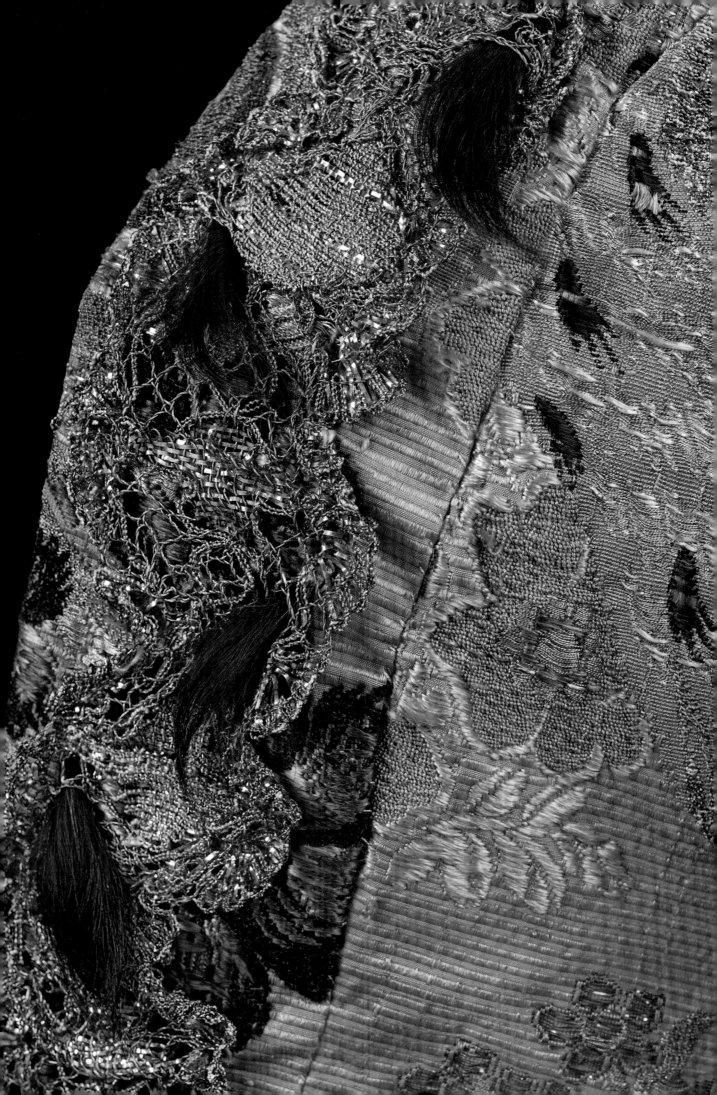

Man's silk coat
French, 1785–90

Given by Mrs R. M. Woods
T.17-1950

'Fake fur' was also fashionable in the eighteenth century, as demonstrated by this eccentrically patterned coat. The imitation 'leopard spot' markings are woven into the pile of the turquoise velvet. Such whimsical patterns were popular in men's fashions of the late 1770s and early 1780s. A portrait of John Campbell, 1st Baron Cawdor, painted by Joshua Reynolds in 1778 shows a similar leopard-spot velvet waistcoat but in a more natural colouring. The same effect could also be achieved with embroidery or a chiné woven pattern.[2]

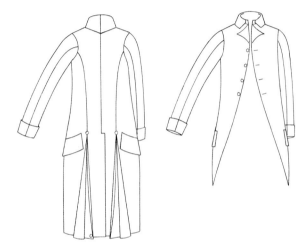

Man's silk waistcoat
Probably British, 1780s

Given by Miss Theophania Fairfax
T.858-1919

Another unusual use of fur (see previous page) can be found on this waistcoat, trimmed with strips of dyed rabbit hair, perhaps to imitate the texture of fringing. The now virulent green colour of the fur may be the result of a chemical change in the dyestuff over time. Unlike the wild stoat, rabbits were abundant throughout Europe, and their fur was therefore inexpensive.

Other decorative features include appliquéd black velvet ribbons embroidered with spangles, foils and pastes. The revers are faced with black velvet; the left one is embroidered with a carnation, and a rose has been worked beside it on the waistcoat.

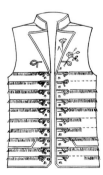
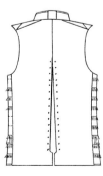

Feathers were another natural material incorporated into eighteenth-century fashionable dress. They are used here – both real and represented – as part of the decoration of this panel for the train of a French court dress or *grand habit*.[3] The cream satin ground is appliquéd with pink silk, as well as mauve and green silk arranged in swags. The embroidery design includes peacock feathers worked in chenille thread, with roses, embroidered separately, cut out and applied to the satin. What look like pearls are padded circles of applied white satin encircled with chenille thread. Swansdown (under-plumage of a swan) edges the swags, some of the silken pearls and the border of the hem, adding texture to the surface.

The *grand habit* was the most formal style of French court dress, comprising a boned bodice (*grand corps*), a petticoat (*jupon*) worn over a wide hoop, and a long train (*bas de robe*) attached at the waist.[4] This panel is only half the train; it would have been sewn to another long panel worked in a mirror image of the embroidery design.

Silk panel for a court train
French, c. 1780

Given by the Royal School of Needlework
T.89–1967

Woman's feather hat
British, 1750–70

T.90-2003

This hat uses inexpensive materials, like the rabbit-fur waistcoat on page 211 (below), in this case feathers from barnyard birds such as roosters and guinea fowl. Some have been dyed bright colours and others left in their natural shades to create a jaunty pattern. The shallow crown and wide brim were a popular style of women's hat in the mid-eighteenth century.

On this petticoat, dyed-blue feathers compete for attention with a medley of other decoration applied to a broad border of silver bobbin lace. The feathers surround maroon silk grosgrain ribbons, folded and arranged in the shape of flowers with a white glass bead marking the centre of each. Loops of floss silk form additional floral elements, and these are joined by lengths of knotted floss silk in shades of green. A matching sack of the same silver-brocaded silk, similarly decorated, accompanies the petticoat; together they made an ensemble of formal evening dress.

Woman's silk petticoat
British, 1760s, of French silk, c. 1755
T.251:A-1959

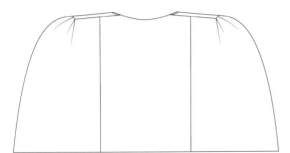 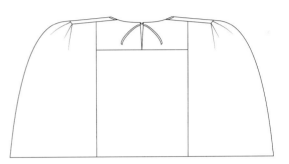

Straw is another humble material that was put to fashionable use in the eighteenth century. Originally a form of protective headwear for agricultural workers, wide-brimmed straw hats with shallow crowns became a stylish accessory for women by the 1740s. The idealized fantasy of the rural idyll held by elite society led to the transformation of certain working-class garments – including the straw hat – into fashionable dress.[5]

The straw plait industry originated in Tuscany, Italy. Leghorn straw, grown in Livorno, north of Genoa, was of the finest quality and was prized for its bright gold colour and the intricate plait local workers made with it. The craft soon spread to other parts of Europe, including Switzerland, Saxony and England.[6] This hat is almost certainly of Italian manufacture, as plaits of such fineness could not be replicated in England until the invention of the straw-splitter tool around 1800. Made from coiled narrow plaits of straw, it is decorated with flowers cut from straw sheets and dyed in a range of colours. Each is outlined with either a fine straw twist or a coloured silk gimp. The base of the hat's shallow crown is encircled with a knotted band of fine linen twine.

Woman's straw hat
Probably Italian, 1760–80

157-1865

Silk pocket book
Probably Italian, 1720–40

Given by C. Stanley Clarke, Esq.
T.29-1915

Because its colour resembled the golden gleam of gilt threads and strip, straw was also used for embroidery. For some of the petals adorning this satin pocket book, straw splints were couched to resemble satin stitch. Other flowers, as well as the heart and bird, were couched with straw-wrapped thread. Silver thread and coloured silks were used for the vase and leaves. Strips of straw in its natural colour as well as dyed red, brown and green define the flowers, winged heart and bird. Fine, two-ply twists of straw were couched around the motifs, and the edges of the pocket book are bound with a narrow silver braid.

C. Stanley Clarke was the son of Caspar Purdon Clarke, director of the V&A from 1896 to 1905. Stanley became the assistant keeper of the Museum's Indian department and over the years donated a number of Southeast Asian objects to the V&A.[7] He gave the Textiles department this beautifully preserved pocket book in 1915, having 'purchased it recently at a curio shop in Fulham'.[8]

Woman's linen and silk shoe
German or Italian, 1750s

Bequeathed by Miss C. M. Slee
T.69-1947

Straw splints couched to a linen upper form the ground of this shoe's design, which is created by coloured silk threads that wrap around the splints. The sunny hue of the straw is enhanced by the yellow satin covering of the heel and the silver embroidery around the edges of the heel quarters. The fineness of the straw splints and the date of the shoes suggest that they were made at one of the European centres of eighteenth-century straw work.

Introduction
1. Aileen Ribeiro, *Dress in Eighteenth-century Europe* (London, 2002), chapter 5: 'Dress and Etiquette'.
2. John Styles, 'Fashion and Innovation in Early Modern Europe', in *Fashioning the Early Modern*, (ed.), Evelyn Welch (Oxford 2017), pp. 53–5.
3. Anne Buck, *Dress in Eighteenth-Century England* (London, 1979), pp. 208–10.
4. Nathalie Rothstein, *Silk Designs of the Eighteenth Century* (London 1996), pp. 17–18; Kimberly Chrisman-Campbell, 'Paisley Before the Shawl: The Scottish Silk Gauze Industry', *Textile History* 33, no. 2 (2002), pp. 162–76.
5. Joseph Collyer, *The Parent's and Guardian's Directory, and the Youth's Guide, in the Choice of a Profession or Trade* (London, 1761), p. 79.
6. Lesley Ellis Miller, *Selling Silks: A Merchant's Sample Book, 1764* (London, 2014), pp. 16–18.
7. Robert Campbell, *The London Tradesman* (London, 1747), p. 189.
8. Collyer, *The Parent's and Guardian's Directory*, p. 190.
9. Peter Thornton, *Baroque and Rococo Silks* (London, 1965), pp. 78–9.
10. Nathalie Rothstein, *Barbara Johnson's Album of Styles and Fabrics* (London, 1987), pl. 11.
11. Herman Van der Wee, 'The Western European Woollen Industries, 1500–1750', in *The Cambridge History of Western Textiles*, (ed.), David Jenkins, vol. 1 (Cambridge, 2003), pp. 469–72.
12. Collyer, *The Parent's and Guardian's Directory*, p. 301.
13. William Henry Crawford, *The Impact of the Domestic Linen Industry in Ulster* (Belfast, 2005); Alastair J. Durie, *The Scottish Linen Industry in the Eighteenth Century* (Edinburgh, 1979).
14. Lorelei Williams and Sally Thomson, *Marlborough Probate Inventories, 1591–1775*, Wiltshire Record Society 59 (2007), pp. 274–7.
15. Collyer, *The Parent's and Guardian's Directory*, p. 182.
16. Arthur Young, *A Six Months Tour through the North of England*, vol. 3 (London, 1770), p. 76; Frederic Morton Eden, *The State of the Poor*, (1797) (London, 1966), p. 557.
17. Jacques Savary des Brulons, *The Universal Dictionary of Trade and Commerce*, (trans.), Malachy Postlethwayt, vol. 1 (London, 1778), pp. 430–31.
18. Beverley Lemire, *Fashion's Favourite: The Cotton Trade and the Consumer in Britain, 1660–1800* (Oxford, 1991).

19. Campbell, *The London Tradesman*, p. 216.
20. Anon., *A General Description of All Trades* (London, 1747), p. 192.
21. Collyer, *The Parent's and Guardian's Directory*, p. 181.
22. Campbell, *The London Tradesman*, p. 147.
23. Anon., *A General Description*, p. 127, and Collyer, *The Parent's and Guardian's Directory*, pp. 180–81; Campbell, *The London Tradesman*, pp. 147–8.
24. Campbell, *The London Tradesman*, p. 152.
25. Ibid., p. 15
26. Ibid., pp. 148–9, 152–3.
27. Ibid., p. 192.
28. Ibid.
29. Ibid.
30. Ibid., pp. 192–3.
31. Collyer, *The Parent's and Guardian's Directory*, p. 275.
32. Ibid., p. 237.
33. Campbell, *The London Tradesman*, p. 263.
34. Ibid., pp. 212–13.
35. Ibid., p. 227.
36. Anon., *A General Description*, p. 134; Campbell, *The London Tradesman*, p. 227.
37. Giorgio Riello, *A Foot in the Past: Consumers, Producers and Footwear in the Long Eighteenth Century* (Oxford, 2006), chapter 6.
38. Campbell, *The London Tradesman*, pp. 217–18; Collyer, *Parent's and Guardian's Directory*, p. 249.
39. Riello, *A Foot in the Past*, pp. 51–7.
40. Campbell, *The London Tradesman*, p. 147.
41. Ibid., p. 213; Beverly Lemire, *Dress, Culture and Commerce: The English Clothing Trade before the Factory, 1660–1800* (Basingstoke, 1997), pp. 65–6.
42. Anon., *A General Description*, p. 162.
43. Collyer, *The Parent's and Guardian's Directory*, p. 212.
44. Michael Snodin, *Rococo: Art and Design in Hogarth's England* (London, 1984); David Irwin, *Neoclassicism* (London, 1997).
45. Moira Thunder, *Embroidery Designs for Fashion and Furnishings* (London, 2014), pp. 8–26.
46. Rosemary Crill, 'Asia in Europe: Textiles for the West', in *Encounters: The Meeting of Asia and Europe, 1500–1800*, (eds) Anna Jackson and Amin Jaffer (London, 2004), pp. 262–71.
47. John Styles, 'What Were Cottons for in the Industrial Revolution?', in *The Spinning World: A Global History of Cotton Textiles, 1200–1850*, (eds), Giorgio Riello and Prasannan Parthasarathi (Oxford, 2009), pp. 307–26.

48. John Irwin, 'Origins of the "Oriental Style" in English Decorative Art', *The Burlington Magazine* 97, no. 625 (April 1955), pp. 106–14.
49. Dawn Jacobson, *Chinoiserie* (London, 1993), p. 135.

1 Pleats, Gathers and Looped Drapery
1. Victoria and Albert Musem Registry, London (hereafter V&A Registry), nominal file R. Brooman White, letter received 10 April 1917.
2. Kendra Van Cleave and Brooke Welborn, '"Very Much the Taste and Various are the Makes": Reconsidering the Late-Eighteenth-century *Robe à la Polonaise*', *Dress* 39, no. 1 (2013), pp. 1–24.
3. J. W. Croker, *Letters to and from Henrietta, Countess of Suffolk, and her Second Husband, the Hon. George Berkeley, from 1712 to 1767: with Historical, Biographical and Explanatory Notes*, vol. 1 (London, 1824), p. 68.
4. Natalie Rothstein (ed.), *Four Hundred Years of Fashion* (London, 1982), p. 21.
5. Ibid.
6. Madeleine Delpierre, *Dress in France in the Eighteenth Century* (London and New Haven, CT, 1997), p. 21.
7. Paul Cornu, *Galerie des modes et costumes français: dessinés d'après nature, 1778-1787*, (Paris, 1911-12?), plate 42 and accompanying text. The plates were published individually between 1778 and 1787 under the title, *Gallerie des modes et des costumes français dessinés d'après nature*. In the early twentieth century, the plates were republished in five volumes titled: *Galerie des modes et costumes français: dessinés d'après nature, 1778-1787 réimpression accompagnée d'une préface par M. Paul Cornu*. The illustrations on page 43 and 44 is from the Cornu volume in the NAL. Collections of the original 18th-century plates from *Gallerie des modes* can be found online: http://gallica.bnf.fr/ark:/12148/bpt6k1056746t?rk=21459;2
8. Illustrated in *Modes et révolutions*, exh. cat., Musée de la Mode et du Costume, Paris (Paris, 1989), p. 43, cat. 10.
9. Van Cleave and Welborn, '"Very Much the Taste"', pp. 1–24; Norah Waugh, *Cut and Construction of Women's Dress, 1600-1930* (London, 1968), diagram xxi.

2 Collars, Cuffs and Pockets
1. Alice Mackrell, *Shawls, Stoles and Scarves* (London, 1986), p. 47.

2. Delpierre, *Dress in France*, p. 19.
3. Alexander Monro, *The Professor's Daughter: An Essay on Female Conduct Contained in Letters from a Father to His Daughter, 1739*, (transcr.), P.A.G. Monro (Cambridge, 1995), p. 6.
4. Mrs Vernon D. Broughton (ed.), *Court and Private Life in the Time of Queen Charlotte: Being the Journals of Mrs Papendiek*, vol. 1 (London, 1887), p. 247.
5. Susan North, 'Object Lesson: The Physical Manifestation of an Abstraction, A Pair of 1750s Waistcoat Shapes', *Textile History* 39, no. 1 (2009), pp. 99–100.
6. Fig. 5 in *Représentation des globes aérostatiques inventés par MM. Montgolfier*, engraved by François Baricolo, 1783-4, etching, illustrated in Sarah Piettre, 'Catalogue des gilets brodés de la collection du Palais Galliera, Paris', MA thesis, Université Paris-Sorbonne, Paris, 2014, p. 191, fig. 3.

5 Stitching and Quilting
1. D. A. Saguto (ed. and trans.), *M. de Garsault's 1767 Art of the Shoemaker* (Williamsburg, VA, 2009), pp. 53–7.
2. Ibid., p. 100.
3. Linda Baumgarten, 'The Layered Look: Design in Eighteenth-Century Quilted Petticoats', *Dress* 34 (2007), pp. 7–16, 29.
4. Clare Rose, 'Quilting in Eighteenth-century London', *Quilt Studies* 2 (2000), pp. 24–5.
5. V&A Registry, nominal file H. P. Mitchell.

4 Lace and Whitework
1. Santina Levey, *Lace: A History* (Leeds, 1983), pp. 49–51.
2. Ibid., p. 68.
3. Ibid., p. 56.
4. Sonia Ashmore, *Muslin* (London, 2012), p. 16.
5. Levey, *Lace*, p. 72.
6. Durie, *The Scottish Linen Industry*, p. 6.

5 Embroidery
1. Edward Maeder (ed.), *'Art of the Embroiderer' by Charles Germain de Saint-Aubin, 1770* (Los Angeles, CA, 1983), p. 42.
2. Leanna Lee-Whitman, 'The Silk Trade: Chinese Silks and the British East India Company', *Winterthur Portfolio* 17, no. 1 (Spring 1982), pp. 21–41.
3. Verity Wilson, *Chinese Dress* (London, 1986), p. 108.
4. Lee-Whitman, 'The Silk Trade', p. 25.
5. Dr Lily Fang Bai, curator at Guangdong Museum, Guangzhou, made this identification when visiting

the Victoria and Albert Museum in 2015.

6. Jean-Paul LeClercq, 'Les Circuits de fabrication et de commercialisation de l'habit à la française', in *Autour des Van Loo: Peinture, commerce des tissus et espionnage en Europe (1250–1830)* (Rouen, 2012), pp. 228–33, and Anon., *A General Description*, p. 162.

7. Irwin, 'Origins of the "Oriental Style"', pp. 106–14.

8. Sylvia Groves, *The History of Needlework Tools and Accessories* (London, 1973), p. 99.

6 Pastes, Foils and Beads

1. Leslie Linder, *A History of the Writings of Beatrix Potter*, (1971) (London, 1987), p. 118.

2. Caroline Crabtree and Pam Stallebrass, *Beadwork: A World Guide* (London, 2002), pp. 20–22.

3. V&A Registry, nominal file Mrs H. Falcke, report by Eric Maclagan, 18 February 1908.

7 Chintz and Painting

1. Rosemary Crill, *Chintz: Indian Textiles for the West* (London, 2008), p. 14.

2. Ibid., pp. 11–13.

3. Stacey Sloboda, *Chinoiserie: Commerce and Critical Ornament in Eighteenth-Century Britain* (Manchester, 2014), p. 1.

4. Ibid., 142; Jacobson, *Chinoiserie*, p. 141

5. The chintz bed hangings and some of their furniture are in the collections of the V&A: bed hangings: 17 to 19-1906,

W.70-1916; furniture: W.70-1916, W.21.1917 to W.30-1917, W.45-1922, W.37-1929, W.42-1936, W.42-1937, W.41-1977, W.99-1978, W.14-1994.

6. Leanna Lee-Whitman and Maruta Skelton, 'Where Did All the Silver Go? Identifying Eighteenth-century Chinese Painted and Printed Silks', *Textile Museum Journal* 22 (1983), pp. 37–40.

7. Ibid., p. 36.

8. Carington Bowles, *The Artist's Assistant* (London, 1775), p. 55.

9. Anon., *Ermina; or, The Fair Recluse*, vol. 2 (London, 1772), p. 111.

10. 'General State of Fashions', *The Fashionable Magazine; or, Lady's and Gentleman's Repository* (September 1786), p. 1.

11. Lesley Ellis Miller, 'Fashion and Personal Adornment', in *Princely Treasures: European Masterpieces, 1600–1800* (London, 2011), p. 178; Edwina Ehrman, 'The Versailles Sash', *Costume* 44 (2010), pp. 68–9.

12. Anon., *Ambulator; or, A Pocket Companion in a Tour Round London* (London, 1796), p. 66.

13. *Manchester Mercury*, 11 May 1762.

14. *Catalogue of Novels, Plays &c, which will be Lent to Read, at 2d. per Volume, by Lockett, at his Printing-Office, High-Street, Dorchester* (1790), p. 20.

8 Pinking and Punching

1. Eliza Hayward and Eliza Fowler, *The Female Spectator*, 6th edn, vol. 3 (London, 1766), p. 161.

2. Janet Arnold, 'A Pink Domino c. 1760–70 at the Victoria and Albert Museum', *Costume* 3 (1969), pp. 31–4.

3. Anon., *The Workwoman's Guide* (Birmingham, 1838), p. 124.

4. Robert Janaway, 'An Introductory Guide to Textiles from 18th and 19th Century Burials', in *Grave Concerns: Death and Burial in England, 1700–1850*, (ed.), Margaret Cox, Council for British Archaeology Research Report, 113 (York, 1998), pp. 25–9.

5. Clare Graham, 'Precious Paperwork', *Traditional Interior Decoration* (October 1987), pp. 141–50.

6. Kung Ho, 'Reverberating Chinese Traditional Folk Art in a Contemporary Context', *History Research* 3, no. 1 (January 2013), pp. 34–43, 36.

7. Nancy Armstrong, *A Collector's History of Fans* (London, 1984), pp. 59–60.

9 Fringes, Ribbons, Tassels and Buttons

1. F. W. Fairholt, *Costume in England*, vol. 2 (London, 1860), p. 168.

2. Natalie Rothstein (ed.), *Barbara Johnson's Album of Styles and Fabrics* (London, 1987), pls 9, 11.

3. Edwina Ehrman, *The Wedding Dress: 300 Years of Bridal Fashions* (London, 2011), pp. 32–4.

4. Sibylle Jargstorf, *Glass Beads from Europe* (Atglen, PA, 1995), pp. 76 and 164.

5. 'A House for a Dandy: Portugal House', at http://mappingbirmingham.blogspot.co.uk/2012/06/portugal-house-new-street.html, 16 June 2012. Many thanks to Sarah Kimball for this information on her ancestor.

6. V&A Registry, nominal file Miss Lawrence.

10 Fur, Feathers and Straw

1. Miller, *Selling Silks*, f.8gr.

2. Kimberley Chrisman-Campbell, *Fashion Victims: Dress at the Court of Louis XVI and Marie Antoinette* (London, 2015), p. 290, Aileen Ribeiro, *Fashion in the French Revolution* (London, 1988), p. 30.

3. Lesley Ellis Miller, 'Les Matériaux du costume de cour', in *Fastes de cour et cérémonies royales: le costume de cour en Europe, 1650–1800*, (eds), Pierre Arizzoli-Clémentel and Pascale Gorguet Mallesteros (Paris, 2009), pp. 85–6.

4. Chrisman-Campbell, *Fashion Victims*, p. 90.

5. Miller, 'Fashion and Personal Adornment', p. 164.

6. Helen Persson, 'Straw, The Blond Goddess: The Adaptation of a Folk Tradition to Fashion', *Costume* 38, no. 1 (2004), pp. 51–2.

7. 'Clarke, Sir Caspar Purdon', *Oxford Dictionary of National Biography*, www.oxforddnb.com/view/article/32424, accessed 20 May 2017.

8. V&A Registry, nominal file C, Stanley Clarke.

Further Reading

In addition to the works cited in the references, the following are useful sources for eighteenth-century dress.

Arnold, Janet, *Patterns of Fashion: Englishwomen's Dresses and their construction, c. 1660–1860* (London, 1964)

Baumgarten, Linda, *What Clothes Reveal: The Language of Clothing in Colonial and Federal America* (New York, 2002)

—, and John Watson, *Costume Close-up: Clothing Construction and Pattern, 1750–1790* (Williamsburg, VA, 1999)

le Bourhis, Katell (ed.), *The Age of Napoleon: Costume from Revolution to Empire, 1789–1815* (New York, 1989)

Bradfield, Nancy, *Costume in Detail, 1730–1930* (London, 1981)

Buck, Anne M. *Women's Costume: The 18th Century*, Picture Book No. 2 (Manchester, 1954)

Burnston, Sharon, *Fitting and Proper: 18th Century Clothing from the Collection of the Chester County Historical Society* (Texarkana, TX, 1998)

Clabburn, Pamela, *Beadwork*, Shire Album No. 57 (Aylesbury, 1980)

Crowston, Clare Haru, *Fabricating Women: The Seamstresses of Old Regime France, 1675–1791* (London, 2001)

Cunnington, C. Willett, and Phillis Cunnington, *Handbook of English Costume in the 18th Century* (London, 1957)

Ewing, Elizabeth, *Dress and Undress: A History of Women's Underwear* (London, 1989)

Elizabeth-Anne Haldane, 'Encounters with Paper Conservation: The Treatment of a Chinese Painted Silk Dress', *Conservation Journal* 49 (Spring 2005), www.vam.ac.uk/content/journals/conservation-journal/issue-49

Halls, Zillah, *Men's Costume, 1580–1750* (London, 1970)

—, *Women's Costume, 1600–1750* (London, 1969)

—, *Women's Costume, 1750–1800* (London, 1972)

Revolution in Fashion: European Clothing, 1715–1815, exh. cat. (New York/Tokyo, 1990)

Maeder, Edward, *An Elegant Art: Fashion and Fantasy in the Eighteenth Century* (Los Angeles, CA, 1983)

Main, Veronica, *Swiss Straw Work: Techniques of a Fashion Industry* (High Wycombe, 2003)

Modes en miroir: la France et la Hollande au temps des Lumières, exh. cat. (Paris, 2005)

Modes et révolutions, exh. cat. (Paris, 1989)

Ribeiro, Aileen, *A Visual History of Costume: The Eighteenth Century* (London, 1983)

—, *The Art of Dress: Fashion in England and France, 1750–1820* (London, 1995)

Roche, Daniel, *The Culture of Clothing: Dress and Fashion in the Ancien Régime* (Cambridge, 1996)

Rushton, Pauline, *18th Century Costume in the National Museums and Galleries of Merseyside* (Liverpool, 1999)

Steele, Valerie, *The Corset: A Cultural History* (New York, 2001)

Styles, John, *The Dress of the People* (London, 2008)

Tozer, Jane, and Sarah Levitt, *Fabric of Society: A Century of People and their Clothes, 1770–1870* (Manchester, 1983)

Waugh, Norah, *Corsets and Crinolines* (London, 1972)

—, *The Cut of Men's Clothes, 1600–1914* (London, 1994)

—, *The Cut of Women's Clothes, 1600–1930* (London, 1987)

baleen Also known as whalebone. Keratin from the mouths of certain species of whales, with a firm yet flexible structure, used in the eighteenth century to reinforce women's stays and sometimes hoops.

banyan A full-length gown with long sleeves, often loosely shaped, worn informally by men and women.

buckram A coarsely woven linen stiffened with glue, used as an interlining.

blonde A type of bobbin lace made with silk threads, undyed or black.

broadcloth A type of fabric woven with yarns made of carded, short-staple wool, shrunk by beating while submerged in water and fuller's earth, then brushed and sheared to create a nap.

brocading Creating a pattern in a weave with one or more discontinuous, supplementary wefts.

cabochon A smooth, polished finish for a gemstone.

calico A collective term in the eighteenth century for cotton fabrics imported from India.

cambric A very fine, sheer linen of plain weave.

changeable A fabric with the warp and weft each in a different colour, known as 'shot' today.

chenille From the French for 'caterpillar', a tufted weft yarn.

chinoiserie Decorative art and design made in Europe imitating the styles and motifs of Chinese art.

chintz Patterned Indian cottons coloured brightly by a complex dyeing technique.

corded quilting A type of quilting using thick threads instead of wadding.

crewel Lightly twisted worsted embroidery thread.

damask A pattern created by the contrast in the reflection of light from warp- and weft-faced satin weaves.

filé Thread of silk wrapped with metal strip.

flounce A deep gathered or pleated frill used to trim women's petticoats.

foil A thin sheet of silver, silver-gilt or enamelled metal, used in embroidery and on buttons.

frisé Metal thread with a crinkled texture.

frock In the eighteenth century, an informal style of man's coat with a turned-down collar.

fugitive dye One whose chemistry is unstable so that the colour changes or diminishes over time.

fulling See **broadcloth**.

gaufrure French term for an embroidery technique that gives a waffled texture.

gimp Trimming made of silk wrapped around a core of linen or cotton.

gown A style of women's eigheenth-century dress with a fitted back. Also a general term for any eighteenth-century dress and used in the plural as a collective term.

holland Fine plain-weave linen, originally imported from Holland.

hoop, hoop petticoat An under-petticoat made of linen reinforced with cane or baleen to create the fashionable silhouettes of eighteenth-century women's dress.

lace A textile structure created with embroidery techniques (needle lace) or by weaving, twisting or plaiting (bobbin lace). In the eighteenth century, 'lace' also referred to narrow woven decorations, now called 'braid'.

last The wooden form on which a shoe or the foot of a boot is made.

lustring A light, plain-weave silk whose surface has been treated to give it crispness and lustre.

mantua A style of eighteenth-century women's dress comprising a bodice with long skirts looped up at the back, worn with a petticoat.

mordant A metallic salt used to fix some natural dyes.

muslin A fine, sheer, plain-weave cotton woven in India, or a linen made to imitate it.

negligée An eighteenth-century synonym for **sack**.

passementerie Term (originally French) for a wide range of trimmings for dress and furnishings, as well as the techniques used to make them.

piecing Where a piece of a garment, such as a sleeve, collar or front, is composed of smaller pieces of fabric sewn together.

purl Short lengths of coiled silver or silver-gilt wire used in embroidery.

quarters The two pieces that make the heel of a shoe.

revers Eighteenth-century term for lapels.

robings The borders of any style of open-fronted women's dress.

sack Also *sac* or *sacque*. A style of eighteenth-century women's dress with two double box pleats at the back.

satin A close warp-faced weave that is constructed to give an unbroken or smooth, lustrous surface.

shape A length of fabric woven or embroidered in the shape of a waistcoat or coat.

sizing Any substance added to a textile to enhance its smoothness, lustre or stiffness, including gum, starch or gelatin.

spangle The eighteenth-century word for sequin.

stomacher A triangular panel to fill in the open front of a mantua, sack or gown.

strip Narrow pieces of metal used in embroidery and brocade.

tambouring Chain stitch worked with a hook, on fabric set in a circular frame.

vermicelli From the Italian word literally meaning 'little worms'; describing a design of squiggly lines.

whitework Embroidery using white thread on a white ground – usually cotton or linen, sometimes incorporating quilting, cording and drawn thread and pulled fabric techniques.

woollen See **broadcloth**.

worsted Yarns made with combed, long-staple wool, very tightly spun; also the fabric woven with them.

Acknowledgements

I am deeply indebted to my colleagues in Conservation for their help with this project. Although always stretched to the nth of their resources, they never fail to come to the rescue of a fragile object and a desperate curator. Many thanks to Jo Hackett and to Katy Smith, who painstakingly conserved the punched silk kerchief on page 176, and to Lucia Burgio in Conservation Science, whose analysis distinguished the cottons from the linens in this book.

I am also very grateful to other V&A colleagues who generously offered their advice and expertise: Clare Browne, Sau Fong Chan, Judith Crouch, Anna Debendetti, Edwina Ehrman, Mark Evans, Avalon Fotheringham, Lesley Miller and Clare Phillips. Many thanks to Kathryn Johnson for her patience and to Blanche Craig and the design team at Thames & Hudson.

I am very grateful to Avril Hart for her expertise and guidance 22 years ago.

The splendid images are the work of Richard Davis, whose colour transparencies have stood the test of time; Henny Clare shot the new additions to the book and Robert Auton did the piedmontese on page 42. Leonie Davis's drawings still look superb, and Deborah Mallinson skilfully created the new diagrams to complement Leonie's work.

Many thanks to colleagues outside the V&A who helped with the identification of objects and techniques: Sonia Ashmore, Rosemary Crill, Kimberly Chrisman-Campbell, Dr Lily Fang Bai and Suzanne Lussier. Mark Wallis at Past Pleasures kindly allowed the inclusion in this book of his splendid 1740s suit, on loan to the V&A.

Picture Credits